ELEMENTARY EDUCATION

CURRICULUM, INSTRUCTION, AND ASSESSMENT

STUDY GUIDE

A PUBLICATION OF EDUCATIONAL TESTING SERVICE

TABLE OF CONTENTS

FOR MORE INFORMATION

Educational Testing Service offers additional information to assist you in preparing for The Praxis Series tests. *Tests at a Glance* booklets and the *Registration Bulletin* are both available without charge (see below to order). You can also obtain more information from our website: **www.teachingandlearning.org.**

General Inquiries

Phone: 609-771-7395 (Monday-Friday, 8:00 a.m. to 8:00 p.m., Eastern time)

Fax: 609-771-7906

Disability Services

Phone: 609-771-7780

Fax: 609-771-7906

TTY (for deaf or hard-of-hearing callers): 609-771-7714

Mailing Address

Teaching and Learning Division
Educational Testing Service
P.O. Box 6051
Princeton, NJ 08541-6051

Overnight Delivery Address

Teaching and Learning Division
Educational Testing Service
Distribution Center
225 Phillips Blvd.
P.O. Box 77435
Ewing, NJ 08628-7435

INTRODUCTION

ELEMENTARY EDUCATION
CURRICULUM, INSTRUCTION, AND ASSESSMENT

This study guide is designed to help you prepare for taking a test that is required by many states as a licensing examination for elementary school teachers. The test is one part of the licensing requirements; this study guide can be a valuable part of your overall preparation for the test. Like other study guides you may have seen, it contains sample questions that are similar to the questions you will encounter on the actual test and it identifies and explains the correct answers to each question (it often explains the incorrect answers as well).

But this guide does much more than provide questions and answers. With its workbook format and with in-depth questions that surround the sample questions, it encourages you to prepare for the test in a comprehensive, thoughtful way. Throughout this book, you will find tips, suggestions, and questions that will make you think: about the skills you need to be an effective teacher; about the knowledge required to be a successful teacher; and about what it means to be a professional teacher today. If you engage with this book, and study every page, you will not only be better prepared to take the test; you will also be better prepared to be a teacher.

WHAT IS THIS TEST?

Elementary Education: Curriculum, Instruction, and Assessment, which is part of The Praxis Series: Professional Assessments for Beginning Teachers®, has been designed by Educational Testing Service (ETS) for prospective teachers of students in the elementary grades. Your state has adopted The Praxis Series tests because it wants to be certain that you have achieved a specified level of mastery in your subject area before it grants you a license to teach in a classroom. Candidates typically have completed a bachelor's degree program in elementary school education; some candidates may have prepared through an alternative certification program.

The Praxis Series tests are part of a national testing program, but they are adopted by individual states. More than 35 states presently use one or more Praxis Series tests. An advantage of taking these tests is that if you want to teach in another state that requires the tests, you can transfer your scores to that state. However, passing scores for all of the tests are set by the states that use them, so if you are planning to apply for licensure in another state, you may discover that passing scores are different than scores in your state. You can find passing scores for all states that use The Praxis Series tests in the *Understanding Your Praxis Scores* pamphlet, available in most college and university education departments, or by calling (609) 771-7395.

WHY DOES MY STATE REQUIRE THIS TEST?

Your state chose this test because it assesses the breadth and depth of content knowledge that your state wants its teachers to possess before they begin to teach. The level of knowledge reflected in the passing score is based on recommendations of panels of teachers and teacher educators in each subject area in each state. The state licensing agency, and in some cases the state legislature, ratifies (or changes) the passing scores that have been recommended by the panels.

HOW IS THE TEST STRUCTURED?

Elementary Education: Curriculum, Instruction, and Assessment is a two-hour, multiple-choice test. It contains 110 questions, each of which has four possible answers (and only one correct answer). There are questions in six content areas: Reading and Language Arts; Mathematics; Science; Social Studies; Arts and Physical Education; and a General Knowledge section that assesses your knowledge of pedagogy (the art and science of teaching). The questions require that you apply knowledge of educational theory and practice to situations that a teacher is likely to encounter in the classroom.

In each of the content areas you will answer questions that test your understanding of curriculum, instruction, and assessment. There are many versions of this test, each containing different questions, but all versions are structured in one of two ways:

1. In some tests, the questions are grouped into the six content areas (all mathematics questions appear together, for example). In these tests, the questions that relate to curriculum, instruction, and assessment are mixed in their order of presentation throughout the content area being tested.

2. In other tests, the questions are grouped under three headings: Curriculum, Instruction, Assessment. In these versions, the questions are mixed by subject area (so a question about assessment in mathematics, for example, might be followed by a question about assessment in music).

You will receive a version of the test by chance; you may not choose. However, every version of the test adheres to the overall guidelines listed above. The chart below summarizes the structure of the test.

TEST-AT-A-GLANCE

● Two hours   ● 110 multiple-choice questions

Content Categories	Approximate Number of Questions	Approximate Percentage of Examination
1. **Reading and Language Arts:** Curriculum, Instruction, and Assessment	38	35%
2. **Mathematics:** Curriculum, Instruction, and Assessment	22	20%
3. **Science:** Curriculum, Instruction, and Assessment	11	10%
4. **Social Studies:** Curriculum, Instruction, and Assessment	11	10%
5. **Arts and Physical Education:** Curriculum, Instruction, and Assessment	11	10%
6. **General Knowledge:** Curriculum, Instruction, and Assessment	17	15%

WHAT DOES IT MEAN TO GET A TEACHING LICENSE?

Licensure in any area—medicine, law, architecture, accounting, and cosmetology—is an assurance to the public that the person holding the license has demonstrated a certain level of competence. The phrase used in licensure is that the person holding the license *will do no harm*. In the case of teacher licensing, a license tells the public that the person holding the license can be trusted to educate children competently and professionally.

Because a license makes a serious claim about the person who has been licensed, licensure tests are usually quite demanding. In some fields, licensure tests have several parts and take longer than one day to complete. Candidates for licensure in any field plan intensive study as part of their professional preparation; some join study groups, others study alone. Preparing to take a licensure test is, in all cases, a professional activity. Because it assesses the entire body of knowledge or skill for the field you want to enter, preparing for a licensure exam takes planning, discipline, and sustained effort. Studying the curriculum, instruction, and assessment components of the subjects above is highly recommended.

HOW IS THIS TEST DIFFERENT FROM OTHER TESTS I HAVE TAKEN?

The Praxis Series tests are different from a final exam or other tests you may have taken because the tests are comprehensive; that is, they cover a whole field or content area, and thus cover material you may have learned in several courses over more than one year. They require you to synthesize information you have learned from several sources, and to understand the subject as a whole. You will also be required to understand fundamental concepts in your field.

As an elementary school teacher, you will need a thorough understanding of all relevant subject areas, their fundamental concepts, and the ways the various concepts of each field fit together. You will also be required to apply your knowledge to situations in the classroom. Because these are tests for licensure to teach, many of the content questions are embedded in pedagogical situations—student work or student performance in the classroom, or planning instructional or assessment strategies of some kind. These are areas that you can review and prepare to be tested on. Moreover, studying for your licensing exam is an excellent opportunity to reflect on your field and to develop a deeper understanding of it before you begin to teach.

WHAT DOES THE TEST MEASURE?

This test measures your understanding of the "content knowledge" needed to teach elementary school. This includes an understanding of important facts and concepts in each of the five specific subject content areas, as well as an understanding of how to teach those facts and concepts. The test does NOT measure your actual teaching ability. Many states choose to measure teaching skill after you have had a chance to work in a classroom for some period of time. They may measure teaching skill in several ways, including observation, videotaped teaching, and portfolio assessment.

The teachers in your field who helped to design and review this test, and the states that require it, believe that knowledge of the subject area is the first requirement for licensing. Teaching combines many complex skills, only some of which can be measured by a single test. This test measures how thoroughly you have grasped the knowledge you will need to be an effective elementary school teacher.

HOW WAS THE TEST DEVELOPED?

The test development process involves many steps. Teachers around the country were asked to judge the knowledge and skills that are necessary for the beginning teacher to possess. College and university professors who teach education courses were asked the same questions. These responses were rank-ordered and sent out to hundreds of teachers to review. All of the responses were analyzed, and a summary of the judgments of these professionals was produced. From their consensus, ETS developed the specifications (the areas of knowledge being tested) for the multiple-choice test which you will be taking. The specifications were reviewed, modified, and eventually approved by teachers. From the test specifications, groups of teachers and professional test developers created test questions.

When your state adopted the test, local panels of practicing teachers and teacher educators met to examine it, question by question, evaluating each question for its relevance to beginning teachers in your state. This is called a "validity study." A test is considered "valid" for a job if it measures what people must know and be able to do on that job. For the test to be adopted in your state, teachers in your state had to judge that it was valid.

These panels of teachers and teacher educators also performed a "standard-setting study." They read through the tests question by question and decided, through a rigorous process, how many questions a beginning teacher should be able to answer correctly. From this study emerged a recommended passing score. The final passing score was approved by your state's Department of Education or legislature.

Throughout the development process, practitioners in the teaching field—teachers and teacher educators—have determined what the test would contain. The practitioners in your state determined which tests would be used for licensure in your subject area, and helped decide what scores you need to achieve to become licensed. This is how professional licensure works in most fields: those who are already licensed oversee the licensing of new practitioners. When you pass the *Elementary Education: Curriculum, Instruction, and Assessment* test, you and the practitioners in your state can be assured that you have the knowledge required to begin practicing your profession.

HOW SHOULD I PREPARE TO TAKE THIS TEST?

This is a serious test and your preparation should reflect the seriousness accorded to a professional licensing examination. Surveys of candidates who did not pass The Praxis Series tests show that their preparation was woefully inadequate: they either did not prepare at all or prepared without rigor. What is required to pass the test is a thorough understanding of educational theory and practice across five academic content areas. This is a demanding task. You are also expected to know how effective teachers would respond to classroom situations, and you are expected to know the theoretical underpinnings of these actions. In other words, you will have to demonstrate that you understand and can appropriately apply the theories that you have studied in your teacher-education program; at the same time, you will be required to show that you know how to conduct yourself as a practicing teacher in a wide variety of classroom scenarios.

This study guide can be a useful part of your overall preparation, but using it alone will not prepare you to successfully pass the test. You must have a solid, deep understanding of the subjects covered on the test and know how you can best teach these subjects to elementary school students. You will probably discover that you will need to review some areas, or fill in gaps in your knowledge of other areas. Teaching at the elementary level is a complex, demanding occupation. As noted above, your state (along with your school district, your principal, your fellow teachers, and the parents of your students) wants to be sure that you possess the skills and knowledge necessary to meet the challenges of classroom teaching. So this is the time to get out your textbooks and class notes and study them systematically. You may also want to find textbooks that are currently used in each subject area by elementary schools in the state where you want to teach and study those as well.

One step in your preparation is to honestly assess what you know. It is quite possible that you know more about some subjects than you do about others. Working through the material in the chapters that follow will give you a better idea of your strengths and weaknesses. You will find a chart at the end of each chapter that provides an opportunity to evaluate realistically both the areas you have mastered and those where you need more preparation. Use these charts. They can point the way to the kinds of additional preparation you will need to undertake in order to pass the test.

SHOULD I STUDY BY MYSELF OR IN A GROUP?

You can successfully prepare for the test by yourself or as a member of a "study group." The important thing is to prepare seriously. Given the amount of preparation that is required, some candidates work in groups so that they can learn from each other. They assign each member of the group a different content area and each person agrees to review the subject in depth. Then the members present to the group the most important points to know about curriculum, instruction, and assessment issues in their subject areas. In some ways, then, each member is a teacher—and each has a specialty in a subject. Of course, this means that you are dependent on the expertise of the others in the group for your own preparation—and that can be risky. If you prepare in a study group, you may want to do additional preparation on your own.

The study method you follow is not as important as the extent of your preparation. You probably know which method will work best for you. Well-informed, well-prepared test-takers are more likely to pass the test. People who "walk in off the street," unprepared, are much less likely to get a passing score.

FACTS ABOUT THE TEST

1. **You can answer the sections of the test in any order.** You can go through the questions from beginning to end, as many test-takers do, or you can create your own "path." Perhaps you will want to answer questions in your strongest field first and move from your strengths to your weaker areas. There is no "right" or "wrong" way. Use the approach that works for you.

2. **There are no "trick questions" on this test**. You don't have to find any hidden meanings or worry about "trick" wording. All of the questions on the test ask about your content knowledge. Choose the answer that seems most likely to you, not the answer that would be true in some unusual, "what if" situation.

3. **Don't worry about "answer patterns."** There is a myth that answers on multiple-choice tests follow patterns. There is another myth that there will never be more than two questions with the same lettered answer following each other. These are both false. Select the answer you think is correct, and don't be concerned about answer patterns.

4. **There is no "penalty" for guessing**. Your test score is based on the number of correct answers you have, but incorrect answers are not counted against you, as they are on the SAT. When you don't know the answer to a question, try to eliminate any obviously wrong answers and then guess at the correct one.

5. **It's OK to write in your test booklet**. You can write on the pages of the booklet, make notes to yourself, mark questions you want to review later, or jot down anything at all. Your test booklet will be destroyed after you are finished with it. No one is going to look at your booklet, so use it in any way that is helpful to you.

TIPS FOR TAKING THE TEST

1. **Put your answers in the right "bubbles."** It seems obvious, but be sure that you are "bubbling in" the answer to the right question on your answer sheet. You would be surprised by how many candidates fill in a "bubble" without checking to see that the number matches the question they are answering.

2. **Understand each question.** Be sure to take the time to thoroughly understand what each question is asking before you try to answer it. Test-takers often forget this basic advice and jump to the answers before they have understood the question— and they end up with the wrong answer, when they could have found the right one with a little more care.

3. **Narrow down the possible answers.** When you are unsure of the correct answer, you can frequently eliminate answers that are not correct. Sometimes you can look at the remaining answers, then back at the question, and see that one is better than another. If you have narrowed your choices down to two possibilities and can't tell which is the correct one, then guess. One of the two is probably the right answer.

4. **Skip the questions you think are extremely difficult.** There are bound to be some questions that you think are hard. Rather than trying to answer these on your first "pass" through the test, leave them blank, and mark them in your test booklet so that you can come back to them. Pay attention to the time as you answer the rest of the questions on the test and try to finish with 10 or 15 minutes remaining, so that you can go back over the questions you left blank. Even if you don't know the answers the second time you read the questions, see if you can narrow down the possible answers, and then guess.

5. **Keep track of the time.** Bring a watch to the test, just in case the clock in the test room is difficult for you to see. Remember that, on average, you have about one minute to answer each of the 110 questions. (You are given two hours to complete the test.) One minute may not seem like much time, but you will be able to answer a number of questions in only a few seconds each. You will probably have plenty of time to answer all of the questions, but if you find yourself becoming "bogged down" in one section, you might decide to move on and come back to that section later

6. **Read all of the possible answers before selecting one.** Read all of the answers and then re-read the question to be sure the answer you have selected really answers the question being asked. Remember that a question containing a phrase like: "Which of the following does NOT . . ." is asking for the one answer that is NOT a correct statement or conclusion. Three of the four possible answers are TRUE statements. You must select the one statement that is FALSE.

7. **Check your answers.** If you have extra time left over at the end of the test, look over each question and make sure that you have filled in the "bubble" on the answer sheet as you intended. Many candidates make careless mistakes that could have been caught if they had checked their answers.

8. **Don't worry about your score when you are taking the test.** No one is expected to get all of the questions correct. Your score on this test is not analogous to your score on the SAT, the GRE, or other similar tests. It doesn't matter on this test

whether you score very high or barely pass. If you meet the minimum passing score for your state, and you meet the other requirements of the state for obtaining a teaching license, you will receive a license. With your score report you will receive a booklet, entitled *Understanding Your Praxis Scores*, that lists the passing scores for your state.

9. **Don't panic.** If you have thoroughly prepared for the test, you are ready for success. Remember that you will probably do your best by staying calm and focussed.

HOW IS THIS STUDY GUIDE ORGANIZED?

There are questions and answers in this study guide, but there is also much more. In fact, the questions and answers are just the beginning. The six chapters that follow correspond to the six areas on which you will be tested: Reading and Language Arts, Mathematics, Science, Social Studies, Arts and Physical Education, and General Knowledge. Here is how each chapter is organized:

 The Specification Specifications are the "spine" of the test. Each specification indicates a skill or proficiency that licensed teachers should possess, either in content knowledge or in pedagogical knowledge. Specifications are based on job analyses of what teachers actually do on the job, on state standards for teachers, and on standards of professional societies. The people who write the test questions base the questions on the specifications. This study guide contains one question for each specification in every content area.

 About the Specification This section links the specification to the subject area. You will find questions here that ask you to think about the specification broadly and to consider how the specification can be applied to the subject in ways that go beyond the content of the sample question.

 Sample Question This is a question that is similar to an actual test question. None of the sample questions in this study guide will appear on a test that you take, but each is representative of a question that has been written for this test (according to the individual specification). The format of the questions, each with four possible answers, is also the format of the questions on an actual test.

 About the Question This section is designed to help you think about the sample question in greater depth than if you were simply answering questions on a sample test. Here you might be asked about the assumptions behind the question or be asked about the knowledge you need to possess in order to answer the question correctly.

 What is the Answer? This provides a space for you to write in the letter of the answer you think is correct. There is only one correct answer for each question. On an actual test, you would fill in, on a separate answer sheet, the "bubble" that corresponds to the answer that you have selected.

Explanation of the Answer The correct answer for each question is identified and explained. For many of the questions, all four answers are explained, so that you can see why the wrong answers are not the best choice.

 Beyond the Question The questions asked here "follow up" and "open up" the sample question. Sometimes you will be asked a question that directly follows from the question (for example: "What might the teacher do next?") and other times you will be asked a much broader question that the sample question suggests (for example: "How would you teach this concept to students in third grade?"). This section encourages you to visualize yourself as a teacher and to think about how the sample question might relate to your classroom teaching.

 Tip Occasionally, throughout the book, you will find "tips." These are pieces of advice for you as a test-taker. Sometimes they relate to a specific question; sometimes they provide advice that can be used productively throughout the study guide and test. Be sure to read the tips as you work through the book and try using them whenever you encounter relevant opportunities.

The goal of this study guide is not to simply help you get the right answers to the sample questions; none of the sample questions will appear on the actual test you take. Rather, the goal is to help you understand the educational issues that are at the core of teaching. To engage with the questions that surround the sample questions is to grapple with subjects of fundamental importance for actual teachers. If you work at understanding these additional questions, and answering them thoughtfully, you will not only be preparing to take this test—you will be preparing to become a professional teacher as well.

This test is not just another hurdle. It's not a final exam and it's not an entrance exam. From the point of view of your state and the taxpayers who will be paying your salary, it is a serious assessment of your readiness to enter a classroom and to take children's futures into your hands. Preparing for this test is preparing to teach.

WHY ISN'T THE TEST ORGANIZED BY GRADE LEVEL?

One of the many reasons that teaching is such a demanding occupation is that teachers have to be able to teach students of different ages, who are at different levels of physical, intellectual, and emotional development. They have to be able to adjust their teaching to accommodate the widely varying needs of their students. In addition, beginning teachers have almost no role in selecting the grade they will teach; they are usually assigned to a grade level.

Imagine that you want to teach kindergarten and that you have little interest in teaching fifth grade. Imagine that you are offered a job teaching fifth grade in a school that you really like; in fact, it's the best school you've ever seen. Fortunately for you, you have been educated to teach beyond kindergarten. When you receive your license as an elementary school teacher, you will be licensed to teach at many grade levels. Your school district needs the flexibility and breadth of expertise that your education and license have provided. Your town may experience a boom in families with young children, and you may be moved from one grade level to another to accommodate the demands of changing demographics. Or your state may pass a class-size reduction initiative for grades K-3, and there may suddenly be a huge need for early-elementary teachers. Your state can't afford to license you to teach only one or two grades. So you have to be knowledgeable about the curricular, instructional, and assessment demands of a range of grades. It's a challenge, but it's only one of the many challenges of teaching elementary school.

Throughout the study guide, you are asked to select a grade that you would like to teach and are then asked to answer questions about the needs of students in that grade, or you are asked about situations that might come up in a class at that grade level. Here is an example: "How would you integrate the teaching of literature and science at the grade level you have selected?" Remember, as you answer these questions, that you should be able to answer for ANY grade level. If you are most interested in teaching third grade, for instance, remember that you may need to be able to answer the question for first grade or fifth grade also. If your answers for other grade levels seem shaky to you, or if you're uncertain about how to answer, that indicates that you should "brush up" on your understanding before you take the test.

HOW DO I USE THE TEST SPECIFICATIONS TO HELP ME PREPARE FOR THE TEST?

The specifications for curriculum, instruction, and assessment are the same across all subject areas. That is, a curriculum specification remains identical but the questions about curriculum in a given subject area will be specific to that particular subject (for example, specification 1A is the same in mathematics as it is in science, but the sample question will relate to the particular discipline).

Your immediate goal is to look at the specifications for the test and decide whether or not you will be able to answer questions created from those specifications—for all of the grade levels that you might be asked to teach as a licensed elementary-school teacher. Here are some questions you should ask yourself as you review the specifications:

1. Do I understand what the specification means?

2. Do I know how the specification relates to my job as a teacher?

3. Can I answer questions about the specification?

4. Do I understand the question that follows the specification?

5. Can I apply the specification to other teaching situations, beyond the one described in the question?

6. What are some other ways that this specification applies to my role as a classroom teacher?

7. What additional information do I need in order to be able to answer other questions that involve this specification in other subject areas?

WHAT KINDS OF KNOWLEDGE DOES THE TEST ASSESS?

The test questions cover the breadth of material a new teacher needs to know. They assess basic understanding of curriculum planning, instructional design, and assessment of student learning. Many questions pose particular problems that teachers might face in the classroom, and some are based on authentic examples of student work. Although some questions concern general issues, most questions are set in the context of the subjects most commonly taught in the elementary school: Reading and Language Arts, Mathematics, Science, Social Studies, Arts (including art and music) and Physical Education. "General Knowledge" questions, designed to test your knowledge of pedagogy, are also included in the test.

Here are some of the topics on which you may be tested:

● Knowledge and understanding of topics dealing with the personal, social, and emotional development of children; language and communication; developmentally appropriate instruction

● Learning theories—for example, behaviorism and cognitive views of learning; problem-solving abilities; higher-order thinking skills; metacognition; constructivism

● Curriculum components—for example, scope and sequence; curricular materials; learning objectives

● General principles of instruction—for example, learner motivation; learning environments; diversity; enrichments and reteachings; procedural skills; planning; conferencing

● Classroom management—for example, organization; discipline; procedures; learner responsibility; interventions

● Evaluation of instructional effectiveness and student progress—for example, using classroom assessments to increase learning and motivation; authentic and traditional assessments; analyzing results; effective assessment practices; measurement

● General issues of professional growth—for example, reflective teaching; collaboration; partnerships with colleagues and community; interactions with parents

WHAT TOPICS CAN I EXPECT IN CURRICULUM, INSTRUCTION, AND ASSESSMENT?

Curriculum topics examine the organization, materials, and resources of each content area and the implications for using them.

(A) Components of curricula and how they are organized

(B) Integration of concepts within each content area, and across content areas, and the pedagogical implications of this integration

(C) Types of curricular materials, media, and resources, such as textbooks and trade books in reading, maps and globes in social studies, measurement equipment in math, equipment and displays in science, and technologies like computer software and videotapes

Instruction topics examine content-specific teaching and learning principles and their application for appropriate and effective instruction.

(A) Methods to identify, assess, activate, and build on the prior knowledge, experiences, and skills that a given group of students brings to learning in each content area

(B) Methods for preparing, evaluating, and justifying instructional activities in each content area and across content areas for a given group of students

(C) Selection of teaching and learning strategies, such as demonstration, cooperative learning, guided oral and silent work, use of journals, graphic organizers, and the inquiry method, that will help individual students and groups of students to see and understand varied topics and concepts

(D) Methods for adjusting instruction to meet students' needs, including corrective and developmental instruction, re-teaching, follow-up, and enrichment instruction

(E) Strategies for motivating and encouraging student success

(F) Theoretical and empirical bases of various methods of instruction

Assessment topics examine content-specific and general assessment and evaluation procedures and the implications for using these procedures appropriately and effectively.

(A) Traditional and standardized testing methodologies, such as standardized tests, basal reader tests, and screening tests, that are appropriate for use in each content area and in general

(B) Informal, classroom-based and nontraditional assessment strategies, such as observation, oral reports, running records, informal reading inventories, portfolios, and performance samples, that are appropriate for use in each content area and in general

(C) Interpretation of data obtained from various assessment strategies in each content area and in general

(D) Anticipation and identification of common points of confusion in the content areas, such as errors, patterns of error, inaccuracies, misconceptions and "buggy" algorithms

CONCLUSION

This test is one part of the process by which you can become a licensed elementary-school teacher. You have already spent many years preparing to become a teacher. It is worth taking the time to prepare to take this test. If you work conscientiously through the pages that follow, you will gain insight into the kinds of questions you will be asked on the test. You will also gain an understanding of what you know and what you need to study before you go into the test center.

Finally, you will gain an understanding of issues and topics that will be useful to you as you begin to teach. In using this study guide, you aren't just preparing to take a test; you are preparing for your profession.

READING AND LANGUAGE ARTS

Curriculum, Instruction, Assessment

1

CURRICULUM

Specification 1A

Identify broad purposes for teaching all content areas and identify purposes for teaching particular topics within each content area. (For example, encouraging self-expression in reading/language arts.)

About the Specification

Your state probably has standards for elementary grade students in language arts. You should have a copy of the standards and should look them over. (One place to find these standards quickly might be the website for your state's Department of Education.)

What are the broad purposes for having children learn language arts in elementary school? Do the purposes stay the same across grade levels or do they change?

_____

_____

Purposes for teaching reading and language arts in upper elementary grades

_____

_____

sample question

During a unit on folktales, a second-grade teacher wants to help students engage in higher-order thinking skills. After the students read *The Little Red Hen*, the teacher asks the students to justify the Little Red Hen's decision to eat the bread herself. Which of the levels of Bloom's Taxonomy does this activity address?

(A) application

(B) analysis

(C) synthesis

(D) evaluation

About the Question

How does this question fit into the specification listed above, about purposes for teaching reading and language arts?_____

_____

TIP: To answer this question, you need to understand the levels of Bloom's Taxonomy and select the level that best matches the scenario presented in the question.

What is the Answer? _____

Explanation of the Answer

Teachers need to understand the specific content they teach, but it is of equal importance that they understand their purposes for teaching the content. In this example, for instance, the teacher is using the story of the Little Red Hen as a way to enhance students' thinking skills. By asking the students to justify Little Red Hen's decision to eat the bread, the teacher's aim is to help students sharpen specific, age-appropriate reasoning.

(A) is not the correct answer. According to Bloom's taxonomy, "application" describes using methods, concepts, principles, and theories in new situations. At this stage, the teacher shows, observes, and facilitates.

(B) is not the correct answer. "Analysis" refers to breaking down a communication into its constituent parts. At this stage, the teacher probes, guides, and acts as a resource.

(C) is not the correct answer. "Synthesis" is defined as putting together constituent elements to form a whole. At this stage, the teacher reflects, analyzes, and evaluates.

(D) is the correct answer. "Evaluation" is the level of this task. In asking the students to "justify the Little Red Hen's decision," the teacher is helping them to reason and make judgments and is encouraging them to develop and defend their decisions based on criteria they establish.

Beyond the Question

Look again at your state standards for reading and language arts in the elementary grades. Examine some of the broad purposes that particularly interest you. What are some of the specific topics that might fall within those broad purposes?

Grade Level _____ Standard _____

Purpose of standard _____

Topic _____

Purpose of topic _____

Topic _____

Purpose of topic _____

Specification	Understand the relationship of subject area "parts" to subject area "wholes" for instructional planning and the instructional implications of these relationships. (For example, the role of phonics in students' total reading behavior.)
1B	

About the Specification

This specification addresses the specific parts (e.g., the units or activities) that you would be teaching in order to achieve some of the larger curricular goals that your students would be expected to meet.

Choose a grade that interests you. Look at a reading or language arts text or curriculum you might use in that grade. What are its units? How are they broken into parts?

Unit _____   Part _____

Part _____

Unit _____   Part _____

Part _____

Unit _____   Part _____

Part _____

If you had to describe to a parent how this textbook is organized, what would you say?

_____

sample question

As part of a language arts program, a teacher takes students on field trips, often reads aloud from books, and equips the classroom with pictures and prints. Which of the following student needs is met by all of these instructional practices?

(A) Facilitated social adjustment

(B) Expanded reading readiness

(C) Increased motor development

(D) Improved auditory ability

TIP: Remember that the correct answer will answer all parts of the question. To answer this question, you need to read it carefully and understand exactly what is being asked. Then look at the four options and select the answer that addresses all parts of the question.

About the Question

Write in your own words what this question is asking you. _____

_____

What is the Answer? _____

Explanation of the Answer

Teachers are expected to understand the relationship of "parts" to "wholes" in the subjects they teach and to apply this knowledge in designing learning activities. In this example, a teacher takes students on field trips, reads aloud from books, and puts pictures up in the classroom. Although these activities have a number of possible benefits for students as part of a language arts program, they are all designed to expand readiness for reading

(A) Facilitating social adjustment refers to helping students learn how to behave appropriately in the classroom, meeting the standards of the teacher and interacting well with peers.

(B) is the correct answer. This teacher is expanding the reading readiness of the students through these "pre-reading" activities.

(C) Increasing motor development describes enhancing physical skills and is not related to reading.

(D) Improved auditory ability might be a side benefit derived from reading aloud from books, but it does not relate to field trips or putting pictures in the classroom.

Beyond the Question

For each of the reading readiness activities listed in the sample question, write down a possible benefit for students from the pre-reading activity.

Field Trips _____

Reading Aloud _____

Pictures in the classroom _____

What are some other pre-reading activities that could be added to those included above? List one benefit of each.

Activity _____ *Benefit* _____

Activity _____ *Benefit* _____

Activity _____ *Benefit* _____

Activity _____ *Benefit* _____

Specification	Understand relationships among concepts both within and across content areas and the instructional implications of these interrelationships. (For example, how is a non-fiction essay constructed? How are "word problems" in mathematics structured?)
1C	

About the Specification

What are some ways of using reading and language arts to strengthen mathematics goals?

How might you relate the concept of parts and wholes across language arts, science, social studies, and mathematics? What kinds of visual materials might you use to make your idea vivid in each content area?

Write down some concepts that you know are related across content areas.

Concept   *Content Area(s) Containing Concept*

_____   _____

Concept   *Content Area(s) Containing Concept*

_____   _____

sample question

A fourth-grade teacher wants her students to find some basic information for a short written report on an American Revolutionary War hero. The students may use encyclopedias, biographical profiles, and the Internet. Which of the following language arts strategies is LEAST likely to be used during this exercise?

(A) location of information using alphabetizing skills

(B) understanding information using skim-reading skills

(C) transcription of information using note-taking skills

(D) long-term recall of information using memorization skills

TIP: Watch for the word "least" in a question. This is always your clue that you must select the option that is the least likely action or strategy of the four possibilities. You must find and select the one answer that stands out as the least appropriate of the four choices presented.

About the Question

How is this question related to the specification?_____

What is the Answer? _____

Explanation of the Answer

Teachers must have an understanding of the relationships among concepts across content areas and how to apply their understanding in developing assignments for students. This question asks about the language arts strategy least likely to be used by students during a social studies assignment. All the possible strategies might be employed, but the question asks which "is LEAST likely to be used."

(A) Locating information in dictionaries and encyclopedias can be quickly done by employing alphabetizing skills. This is a strategy that is likely to be employed in this assignment.

(B) Skim reading is always helpful when doing any kind of research. It allows students to determine relevancy of material without having to read every word.

(C) Note-taking skills are needed here to take essential information from the book or website before writing the report.

(D) is the correct answer. Although memorization skills can be important, the assignment here is to write a short report, so long-term recall by commitment to memory is not the goal.

Specification

1D | *Identify types and uses of curricular materials, media and technologies, and other resources. (For example, story books, videos, and subject-related software.)*

About the Specification

What resources besides books are available to the elementary teacher of reading and language arts? (If you don't know, visit an elementary school in the district near your school of education.)

Materials available _____

Media available _____

Technology available _____

How would you find out what Internet resources are available to teach any given lesson in reading and language arts? _____

_____

How might you use the Internet in a lesson with second or third graders?_____

_____

sample question

At the beginning of the school year, a teacher observed that a first-grade reader was unable to use beginning and final consonants correctly. Which of the following instructional resources is most likely to assist the student in developing these skills?

(A) Using "Big Books" and modeling words in context

(B) Showing a video of a popular children's story

(C) Teaching phonics and phonemes in isolation

(D) Displaying pictures and corresponding printed words around the room

TIP: You will encounter many questions on this test in which you are asked to provide an answer that is most likely to solve a problem that is being presented. Basically, you are being asked for the BEST solution. Several of the possible answers are likely to be of some help, but only one will be clearly the best. This is the answer to look for. Remember to ask yourself before you select an answer: "Is this the best answer to the situation presented in this question?"

About the Question

What are "Big Books" and what is their purpose? _____

_____

What is "phonics"? _____

What is "phonemic awareness"? _____

What is "decoding"? _____

What is the Answer? _____

Explanation of the Answer

Teachers have to be able to use curricular materials, media and technologies, and other resources appropriately to help students learn. In this example, a student needs assistance in using beginning and final consonants correctly. One of the four possible activities is most likely to assist the student in developing these skills.

(A) is the correct answer. Using "Big Books" and modeling words in context are techniques that are most likely to be successful in assisting this student. "Big Books" allow teachers to call attention to words in stories and to pronounce these words for students, all in the context of the stories. Teachers can also engage students in pronouncing words in the stories.

(B) Although showing a video might have other benefits, it is not likely to assist this student with the need to develop better skills in using beginning and final consonants correctly.

(C) Explicit phonics instruction can be effective, but it is not as likely to lead to success for this student as using "Big Books" and modeling words in context.

(D) Displaying pictures and corresponding words in the classroom will be helpful for some students who are having problems matching words and images, but it is not a practice that is targeted to assisting this student who is having difficulty with beginning and final consonants.

Beyond the Question

Think about the various learning styles that you will encounter in an elementary school language arts class. What kinds of curricular materials, materials, and technology might be most appropriate for these learning styles?

Visual Learners   _____

Auditory Learners   _____

Sensory Learners   _____

Kinesthetic Learners   _____

As a beginning teacher, you will probably be asked to teach an existing language arts curriculum. Choose a grade level that you think you want to teach, and look back over the state standards and the textbook(s) you examined. Are there aspects of the curriculum or its component parts that you think you need to know more about?

_____

_____

How could you learn about these topics or units?

_____

_____

Looking at this specification, are there any grades for which you feel less prepared to use developmentally appropriate materials, media, or technology?

If so, why?_____

_____

What can you do to become better prepared?   _____

_____

Specification

2A

Demonstrate knowledge of methods of identifying, assessing, activating, and building on the students' prior knowledge, experiences, cultural backgrounds, and skills in language arts.

About the Specification

Knowing your students' prior knowledge and skills in any area is an important part of understanding the students and it is a foundation for effective teaching.

Think of a unit that you might be starting in a language arts class (introducing a book, for example, or beginning to write creatively). What are three ways you could determine your students' prior knowledge, experiences, and skills before beginning the unit?

1. _____

2. _____

3. _____

sample question

At the end of a second-grade reading unit, you read the following sentences in a response journal from one of your students:

> I liked the story. The boy wds a good suh.

The student will need help with which of the following?

(A) Synonyms

(B) Antonyms

(C) Phonics

(D) Homophones

About the Question

What are synonyms? _____

What are antonyms? _____

What are homophones? _____

Why is it useful for a language arts teacher to know these terms? _____

_____

What is the Answer? _____

 ## Explanation of the Answer

In the scenario presented here, the student has confused the word "son" (which is the desired word) with the word "sun," a word that sounds the same. To find the answer, you must identify the term for words that sound the same but have different meanings.

(A) Synonyms are words that have similar meanings, not words that sound alike.

(B) Antonyms are words that have opposite meanings, not words that sound alike.

(C) Phonics is the overall term given to the teaching of reading and pronouncing words by "sounding out" the phonetic values of letters and syllables.

(D) is the correct answer. Homophones are words that sound alike but have different meanings or spellings.

Beyond the Question

What kind of help could the teacher offer this student in regard to understanding and correctly using homophones? _____

_____

Specification	Demonstrate knowledge of methods of preparing, evaluating, and justifying instructional activities within and across content areas.
2B	

About the Specification

This specification is at the core of teaching. It is about preparing and conducting the actual instruction, evaluating whether the instruction "worked" for students, and judging it against goals.

What is the difference between students being "on task" and students being "engaged" in an activity? _____

_____

_____

A class has completed the reading of a novel. Which of the following actions by the teacher is most likely to foster continued interest in the reading of fiction?

(A) Calling on students to answer questions about the story's theme and setting

(B) Having small groups of students discuss what they liked and disliked about the story

(C) Telling students that there will be a follow-up assignment to compare the story with other stories they have read

(D) Asking students to prepare a graphic organizer that shows the relationship between story parts

TIP: Remember to apply your knowledge about students. In approaching this question, for example, you might ask yourself: "What do I know about motivating students?" You certainly know that students who are engaged with their own learning are more likely to want to continue to learn. You can apply what you know by looking for the activity that is most likely to engage students in learning.

About the Question

How is the question related to the specification? _____

_____

What is a possible drawback to the teacher's engaging only in (B) as a method for assessing reading comprehension?_____

_____

What is the Answer? _____

Explanation of the Answer

Teachers must always be aware of the consequences of the learning activities they select. In this question, for example, the teacher might have chosen any one of these actions to follow up the reading of the novel. However, one of these activities is most likely "to foster continued interest in the reading of fiction." This is an example of applying knowledge of student motivation strategies to a specific action in the classroom.

(A) Calling on students to answer questions about the story's theme and setting might be a useful way to assess their understanding, but it is not the best option for fostering ongoing interest.

(B) is the correct answer. Discussion in class about what students liked and disliked about the story is the most likely of the options to foster continued interest in the reading of fiction. A class discussion that includes students describing what they liked and disliked about the story is the most involving of the possible activities.

(C) Telling students about a follow-up assignment is unlikely to foster their interest in reading other fiction.

(D) Asking students to prepare a graphic organizer is a method of assessing whether they understand the relationship of the story parts, but it is not likely to foster continued interest in reading fiction.

Beyond the Question

What are some other ways of fostering interest in the reading of fiction?

_____

_____

Specification 2C	Select teaching and learning strategies to help individual students or groups of students understand topics and concepts within content areas. (For example, demonstration; cooperative learning; guided oral and silent work; use of journals and logs; graphic organizers; and inquiry method.)

About the Specification

What is the relationship between different kinds of learning styles and teaching strategies? _____

_____

sample question

After completing a unit on reading newspapers, a teacher discovers that several students still don't understand some of the key principles of newspaper articles. These students are given two sets of cards to match. One set contains headlines and the other contains news articles. Which of the following skills are students most likely to develop as a result of this activity?

(A) Decoding text

(B) Recognizing sight vocabulary

(C) Identifying main ideas

(D) Using context clues for word meaning

About the Question

Newspapers can be excellent teaching tools, useful for many purposes. Can you identify some ways in which a language arts teacher might use newspapers in the classroom? _____

_____

Explanation of the Answer

The most successful and effective teachers always keep their learning objectives in mind. Although they have a variety of techniques that they can draw on, they don't vary their techniques just to keep students from getting bored. Instead, they use the strategies that are the most useful in facilitating their students' learning. Here you are asked about the skills that are most likely to be developed as a result of a specific activity. Another way to look at this question is to ask: "What is the goal of this assignment?"

(A) Decoding text refers to a reading skill and does not describe a skill that is likely to be developed as a result of this activity.

(B) Recognizing sight vocabulary is also unlikely to be developed by this activity.

(C) is the correct answer. Identifying main ideas is the likely result of this activity. Newspaper headlines usually summarize the main ideas of the articles they describe.

(D) Using context clues for word meaning is a reading skill, but it is unlikely to be enhanced by this particular activity.

Beyond the Question

What other activities might help students identify main ideas in non-fiction prose? _____

_____

Specification	Demonstrate knowledge of methods of adjusting instruction to
2D	meet students' needs. (For example, corrective and developmental instruction; re-teaching; follow-up and enrichment instruction; and preparation of content area instruction to meet the needs of all readers.)

About the Specification

The students in any elementary school classroom have differing sets of skills in reading and language arts. There will be readers at grade level, for example, along with readers below and above grade level. If you were teaching, how would you facilitate learning for students at different stages of reading development?

_____

_____

sample question

A first-grade student wrote, "R dg is bg n blk" and read aloud: "Our dog is big and black." Which of the following instructional activities is most likely to assist the student in becoming a more competent speller?

(A) discussion of the difference between "our" and "are"

(B) demonstration of left to right movement

(C) explicit instruction in phonics and phonemic awareness

(D) reviews of the rules of capitalization and punctuation

About the Question

Early elementary students often have difficulties learning to spell. How can teachers help students become more competent spellers?

What is the Answer? _____

Explanation of the Answer

Analyzing student work can provide valuable insights into what a student can do and what additional work and activities are needed. A teacher needs to select developmentally appropriate strategies and adjust instruction accordingly to meet the needs of individual students.

In this question, a first-grade student writes the words phonetically, as they are heard and not as they are spelled. You are asked which of the activities listed is most likely to offer assistance to this student.

(A) Although discussing the difference between "our" and "are" addresses one problem, it is not developmentally appropriate for a student of this age and ability.

(B) There is no evidence that the student is having problems with left to right movement.

(C) is the correct answer. Of all the options presented, "explicit instruction in phonics and phonemic awareness" is most likely to assist the student in becoming a better speller.

(D) Although reviewing the rules of capitalization and punctuation might be useful at a later time, it is instruction in phonics that is needed now.

Beyond the Question

If you had a first-grade class with children spelling at grade level, and children below and above grade level, how would you structure your class's spelling program to best meet the needs of all learners? _____

_____

| Specification | Demonstrate knowledge of various strategies for motivating students and encouraging their success. (For example, praise, wait time, and token economies.) |

2E

About the Specification

Motivation is essential to student success. Can you give examples of how you might motivate students to read? _____

_____

sample question

Some teachers require their students to give oral book reports. Which of the following is the best rationale for using oral book reports to motivate students to read?

(A) They provide students with practice in making formal presentations before a group.

(B) They show that students have read the books and know the plots.

(C) They require students to analyze every book they read.

(D) They encourage students to share their reading experiences with others.

About the Question

Reading and writing are often very difficult for students in elementary school, and students can become frustrated with both. What are the positive and negative effects or requiring oral book reports of all students? _____

_____

_____

What is the Answer? _____

Explanation of the Answer

Motivating students and encouraging their success are critical parts of successful teaching. Teachers, even beginning teachers, are expected to be familiar with motivational strategies. This question asks about oral book reports, and the rationale for requiring students to present their reports orally, but it is really a question about what motivates students to read. It does not ask about other positive outcomes from oral presentations. It asks which is the most likely motivator for reading.

(A) Oral book reports do provide children with practice in making formal presentations before a group, but this is not the best rationale for motivating students to read.

(B) Oral book reports also show that children have read the books and know the plots but, again, this not the best rationale for motivating students to read.

(C) Oral book reports do not require children to analyze every book they read. Even if they did, this would not be the best motivator for student reading.

(D) is the correct answer. Oral book reports encourage children to share enjoyable reading experiences with others. This is a prime motivator for both the students who present reports and for the students who hear them.

Beyond the Question

What are some different ways that oral book reports can be structured to appeal to all students in the class, ensuring that book reports do contribute to students' motivation to read? _____

_____

What are some other ways that students can share with each other about books they have read? _____

_____

Specification	Demonstrates knowledge of a variety of approaches to instruc-
2F	tion and the theoretical and empirical bases of these approaches. (For example, developmentally appropriate instruction and model-based classroom management.)

About the Specification

What approaches to instruction have you learned? What theories and theorists do you associate with these approaches?

Instructional Approach   _Theories/Theorists_

_____   _____

_____   _____

What theorists have made the most difference in your thinking about teaching children? Why? _____

_____

_____

_____

In a classroom where a teacher keeps records of students' oral language and provides opportunities for shared, individualized, and guided reading, which of the following philosophies is utilized?

(A) Hunter's work on effective teaching

(B) Piaget's work on child development

(C) Johnson and Johnson's work on cooperative learning

(D) Holdaway and Clay's work on literacy development

About the Question

What is "shared reading"? _____

What is "individualized reading"? _____

What is "guided reading"? _____

What is the Answer? _____

Explanation of the Answer

In addition to being able to use a variety of appropriate techniques in their teaching, teachers should be familiar with the theoretical bases of their approaches. This question asks candidates to demonstrate their knowledge of theory by presenting a teaching technique and inquiring about the theory that is being put into practice. It is not enough to be able to recite or name the work of theorists; candidates must understand the classroom applications of theories.

(A) is not the correct answer. After years of observing classroom instruction, Madeline Hunter outlined seven basic components of a good lesson plan. The seven steps detail the fundamentals of developing a sequence of lesson planning.

(B) Jean Piaget's work on child development describes stages of cognitive development through which children pass on their way to adulthood. He states that all children develop cognitively in the same manner, progressing through four stages, which he calls: Sensorimotor (from birth to about age 2); Preoperational Thought (about 2 to 6 or 7 years); Concrete Operations (about 6 or 7 to age 11 or 12); and Formal Operations (from 11 or 12 to adult).

(C) Roger and David Johnson's work on cooperative learning revolves around the instructional use of small groups. They believe that any assignment in any curriculum can be structured for cooperative learning groups. In these groups, students have two responsibilities: to learn the assigned material and to be sure that other members of the group also learn.

(D) is the correct answer. Donald Holdaway and Marie Clay's work on literacy development shows the positive effects of keeping records of students' oral language and providing opportunities for shared, individualized, and guided reading.

Beyond the Question

You should be familiar with the work of all of the theorists above. Be prepared to answer questions like the following:

According to Piaget, what are the characteristics of children who are in the "Concrete Operations" stage? _____

_____

According to the Johnsons, what factors must be present to ensure the success of cooperative learning? _____

_____

ASSESSMENT

Specification **3A**	*Demonstrate knowledge of when and how to use traditional and standardized testing methodologies. (For example, standardized tests, publisher-produced tests, screening tests.)*

About the Specification

What kinds of traditional and standardized tests for reading and language arts do you know? _____

_____

What does "standardized test" mean? _____

_____

For what purposes can standardized tests be useful? _____

_____

sample question

In order for a language arts teacher to make comparisons of current students with other students from the same state in vocabulary, language mechanics, and reading comprehension, the teacher would need to consult which of the following?

(A) Standardized test results

(B) Last year's report cards

(C) IQ test scores

(D) IEPs

About the Question

Are IQ test scores useful for teachers? _____

_____

Why or why not? _____

What are IEPs? _____

For what purpose are they used? _____

What is the Answer? _____

Explanation of the Answer

Assessment and evaluation procedures are a critical component of teaching. Teachers need to be able to assess their students' progress in order to plan assignments and classroom lessons. Effective teaching is often the result of effective assessment. As a test-taker, you will be asked to demonstrate your knowledge of when and how to use traditional and standardized tests. This question asks which type of assessment would allow this language arts teacher to make comparisons of students in specific classes with other students from the same state who have taken similar classes.

(A) is the correct answer. Standardized test results report the performance of students, and groups of students, all of whom have taken the same test or tests. This is the kind of information this teacher needs.

(B) Last year's report cards could allow the teacher to see how individual students performed in similar subjects last year, but would not allow comparisons with other students in the state.

(C) IQ test scores are not relevant for the kinds of comparisons the teacher wants to make.

(D) Individualized education plans (IEPs) describe plans for specific students and are not relevant to the goals of this teacher.

Beyond the Question

Assessment is actually just information gathering. In order for assessment to be valuable, the teacher has to do something with it. What might the teacher do with the information provided by the standardized tests in the question above?_____

_____

Why do states give standardized tests like the one described? _____

_____

To whom should the test results go, and what might they reveal? _____

_____

| Specification | Demonstrate knowledge of various classroom-based, informal, or nontraditional assessment strategies. (For example, observation; oral reports; running records; informal reading inventories; portfolios; and performance samples.) |

3B

About the Specification

Are you familiar with the kinds of assessments described in the specification? Think about how you might describe each type.

What other kinds of informal or nontraditional assessments could you imagine using for reading? _____

sample question

A third grader wrote a self-evaluation as part of the writing portfolio that was assembled at the end of the year.

"I specially like this pice. I worked real hard on making it intresting and showing alot of pixtures with my work. This pice shows me being persistint. Now that I am allmost done with third grade I see me as a real writer. When I first start a new story I feel like I weigh 200 pounds. When I'm allmost done I feel like a soaring bird.

P.S. It has been a great year in 3rd grade!"

Which of the following best assesses this student as a third-grade writer?

(A) The student continues to rely heavily on invented spelling rather than standard spelling in his writing.

(B) The student has a very negative attitude toward the writing process and finds it to be very laborious.

(C) The student's writing skills are adequately developed for the grade level.

(D) The student's organizational skills in thinking and writing are poorly developed.

TIP: There are no "trick questions" on this test. Remember not to "overread" questions or look for hidden meanings. One useful way to approach a question like this is to read the handwritten passage and then evaluate each statement to see if it seems to you to be true or false. The one true statement is the correct answer to the question.

About the Question

What is this self-evaluation designed to assess? _____

Explanation of the Answer

Assessment takes place in many ways. Here you are asked to look at a hand-written self-evaluation from a third-grade student, which was developed as part of a writing portfolio assembled at the end of the year. The question asks which of the four evaluative statements best assesses this student as a writer. Your task here is to read the sample and to evaluate it as if you were the teacher.

(A) While this student relies on temporary spelling, this answer does not address the student as a whole. The student does not "rely heavily on invented spelling."

(B) It is certainly not true that "The student has a very negative attitude toward the writing process and finds it to be very laborious." In fact, the student seems to enjoy writing.

(C) is the correct answer. "The student's writing skills are adequately developed for the grade level." This is a clear evaluative summary.

(D) It is not true that "The student's organizational skills in thinking and writing are poorly developed." Keeping the grade level in mind, the student's skills in thinking and writing appear, from this sample, to be adequately developed for grade level.

Beyond the Question

In what ways can a teacher help students evaluate their own work fairly and accurately? _____

_____

Specification	Interpret data obtained from various formal and informal assessments
3C	

About the Specification

Assessment is data collection. Interpreting data from "various formal and informal assessments" should give you an overall sense of a student's current knowledge and skill levels. Its purpose is to assist you in developing teaching that is appropriate for that student.

What kinds of data do you get from an in-class, timed writing sample? _____

_____

What kinds of data do you get from a process writing sample? _____

_____

What kinds of data do you get from an hour-long multiple-choice test? _____

_____

A fourth-grade teacher has students use portfolios to keep all their language arts essays for the marking period. This method of assessment can best help the teacher determine which of the following?

(A) A student's understanding of a specific assignment.

(B) A student's probable stanine on a language arts standardized test.

(C) A student's general development in writing skills over the time period.

(D) A student's ability to turn in on-time work for future writing assignments.

What is the Answer? _____

Explanation of the Answer

There are many types of non-traditional assessments, including observation, oral reports, and running records. Here a fourth-grade teacher has students use portfolios for all their essays. By using portfolios, the teacher can assess their performance over the entire marking period. You are to identify what the teacher can best determine about his students' abilities from the portfolios.

(A) Understanding a specific assignment is not the purpose of portfolios. Assessing growth and development of skills and abilities over a period of time is their primary value.

(B) Standardized test scores do not necessarily correlate with work entered into portfolios. They are not generally used to predict future performance.

(C) is the correct answer. General development of skills and abilities over a period of time is the main value of student portfolios.

(D) Portfolios can give the teacher an idea of a student's past record but cannot predict a student's future performance.

Beyond the Question

What benefits might this teacher see if he or she had asked students to select the work that went into their portfolios?_____

_____

How else might the teacher have used portfolios in assessing student progress in language arts? _____

_____

_____

Specification	Identify common points of confusion or misconception among elementary school learners in the various content areas. (For example, errors and patterns of errors.)
3D	

About the Specification

Name 3 common points of confusion or misconceptions you are likely to see in new readers (in first or second grade):

1. _____

2. _____

3. _____

Name 3 common points of confusion or misconceptions you are likely to see in the writing of fourth- and fifth-graders:

1. _____

2. _____

3. _____

sample question

The example below is typical of one student's work when asked to produce a writing sample.

Me and my Mom are great buddies. We always go so many fun places together. Just yesterday a friend of ours gave my Mom and I tickets to a terific baseball game.

The teacher can best help this student's writing by reviewing which of the following with the student?

(A) syntax

(B) verbs

(C) pronouns

(D) spelling

About the Question

What is syntax? _____

What kinds of problems do children at the age of the student in this question typically have with verbs? _____

_____

What is the Answer? _____

Explanation of the Answer

Students make errors in their work that sometimes are random but, at other times, show a "pattern" or a "common point of confusion" shared among other students. Here your task is to read the sample work and determine what type of review would BEST help the student who wrote it.

(A) The syntax, or word order, is not much of a problem in this sample.

(B) The verbs are well used. They generally agree with the subjects and are in the correct tense.

(C) is the correct answer. The student has made some errors in pronoun usage, confusing subjective pronouns (I, he, she, we, etc.) with objective ones (me, him, her, us, etc.). A review of proper usage of each type of pronoun as well as their word order placement (my Mom and I) would best help this student's writing.

(D) The student has made only one spelling error in this sample ("terific").

Beyond the Question

What are some ways in which you can help students overcome common misunderstandings of grammar, syntax, and spelling? _____

_____

_____

_____

_____

_____

_____

_____

PUTTING IT ALL TOGETHER

READING AND LANGUAGE ARTS

Now that you have worked through this section of the workbook, you should have a general idea of what curriculum, instruction, and assessment issues are likely to appear on the test. The following chart is intended to help you think about the areas in which you might need further review before you take the test.

In addition, here is a list of topics that might appear on the test in the context of curriculum, instruction, and assessment in this subject area. Can you answer questions on these topics?

Sample Topics

- Readiness factors in reading and writing

- Strategies for word recognition

- Comprehension

- Strategies for locating and using information

- Major approaches to and effective strategies for the teaching and assessment of reading, listening, speaking, and writing

- Analysis of students' work samples

- Children's literature

- Integration of reading and language arts

- Appropriate planning and instructional techniques to enhance students' literacy growth

If you are working in a study group, you might try asking each other questions on these topics. You might also challenge each other to come up with questions based on the topics and on the specifications that appear throughout this section.

STUDY PLAN: READING AND LANGUAGE ARTS

Content areas I need to study	Materials I have	Materials I need	Where can I find material I need?

MATHEMATICS

Curriculum,

Instruction,

Assessment

Specification 1A | *Identify broad purposes for teaching all content areas and identify purposes for teaching particular topics within each content area.*

About the Specification

Look at the mathematics standards for elementary school students in your state (which should be readily available at a college or university education department or from the Internet). What are the general purposes—the broad goals—for teaching mathematics at the elementary school level; that is, what should students take away with them when they leave elementary school?

_____

_____

Choose one of these general purposes for teaching mathematics in elementary school.

_____

_____

What are some mathematics topics that help accomplish that purpose?

_____

_____

_____

The following are tasks that teachers might ask students to perform.

I.   Adding 2 + 4

II. Joining 2 blocks and 4 blocks

III. Adding 2 apples + 4 apples, which are shown in a picture

IV. Solving $x + 4 = 6$

In which of the following sequences are the tasks ordered from the most concrete level to the most abstract level?

(A) II, I, III, IV

(B) II, III, I, IV

(C) III, I, II, IV

(D) III, II, IV, I

TIP: One approach to answering this type of question is to put the items into the order that you think is correct (you can write this down in your test booklet too) and then look over the possible answers to see which one has the same order. This saves time in evaluating each of the possible answers.

About the Question

How does the question relate to the specification (i.e., how does knowing which activities are more concrete and which are more abstract relate to understanding the broad purposes of teaching mathematics in elementary school?

_____

_____

What is the Answer? _____

Explanation of the Answer

Mathematics teachers need to understand the skills that are required to perform mathematical tasks and they need to know the order in which their students can be expected to learn them. In this question you are presented with four tasks and asked to rank them from the "most concrete" to the "most abstract." Note that each of the tasks is preceded by a Roman numeral. The four possible answers each contain the four Roman numerals, but in a different order.

(B) is the correct answer. The most "concrete" task is one that involves physical manipulation, joining two blocks and four blocks. Moving toward an abstract level, the next task is a graphic representation, adding apples shown in illustrations. Next is numeric, adding two numbers. The most abstract of the four tasks is solving for the unknown, here represented as x.

Beyond the Question

Choose one of the general purposes that particularly interests you from the list you created above. _____

_____

Choose a grade level that interests you. _____

What topics would you teach to children at that grade level to contribute to the more general purpose of teaching mathematics?

_____

_____

What must children already know and be able to do in order to learn the topics you listed above?

_____

_____

Specification 1B	Understand the relationship of subject area "parts" to subject area "wholes" for instructional planning and the instructional implications of these relationships. (For example, addition used in multiplication.)

About the Specification

What are general mathematics topics in the grade level you said above you are interested in teaching? (If you don't know what these topics are, look in a textbook or workbook or teacher's manual for that grade level.)

_____

_____

What are some of the "parts" of those topics?

General Topics	_"Parts" of Each Topic_
_____	_____
	_____
	_____
_____	_____
	_____
	_____

Which of the following problems requires the most advanced understanding of the relationships between arithmetic operations?

(A) 27 + 36 = 30 + 33 = 63

(B) 7/8 + 9/10 is about 2

(C) 1/2 divided by 2/3 = 1/2 x 3/2 = 3/4

(D) 105 – 69 = 36

About the Question

What does "advanced understanding" mean in this question? _____

_____

Put into your own words what the question is asking. _____

_____

What is the Answer? _____

Explanation of the Answer

Arithmetic operations are an important part of elementary-school mathematics. Here, again, teachers must understand the developmental hierarchy of skills needed to solve various kinds of problems. There are four problems presented and solved in this question. Your task is to identify the problem that requires the greatest understanding of the relationships of arithmetic operations.

(C) is the correct answer. Dividing and multiplying fractions requires the most advanced understanding and the highest-order mathematics skills. It is a more complex task than adding fractions (B) or either of the options that involve adding whole numbers (A and D).

Beyond the Question

Choose a different grade level than the one you chose earlier. If you chose an upper elementary grade, choose a lower one this time, and vice versa.

Grade level: _____

What topics in mathematics would you be teaching students at that grade level? (Again, you may need to look at a textbook, workbook, or teacher's manual from that grade level.)

_____

_____

What would students need to know and be able to do before they could learn the topics you would be teaching at this grade level? _____

_____

Specification

1C

Understand relationships among concepts both within and across content areas and the instructional implications of these interrelationships. (For example, use of estimation in a variety of problem solving situations.)

About the Specification

For students in the grade(s) you would most like to teach, what mathematics skills would you like to see them using in

Social studies _____

Science _____

Art _____

Other content areas _____

sample question

The goal of a particular mathematics curriculum is that students will use computational strategies fluently and estimate appropriately. Which of the following objectives for students best reflects that goal?

(A) Students in all grades will use calculators for all mathematical tasks.

(B) Students in all grades will be drilled daily on basic number facts.

(C) Students in all grades will know the connections between the basic arithmetic operations.

(D) Students in all grades will evaluate the reasonableness of their answers.

About the Question

Why is it important for students to "use computational strategies fluently and estimate appropriately"? _____

_____

How can teachers help students reach this goal? _____

_____

What is the Answer? _____

Explanation of the Answer

Curriculum goals must be incorporated into classroom teaching. Teachers must be able to develop objectives that help their students meet the overall goals. Here the goal is to use computational strategies accurately and to estimate appropriately. You are asked to identify which of the objectives offered best reflects that goal.

(D) is the correct answer. To "evaluate the reasonableness of their answers," students must understand the computational strategies involved in mathematical solutions before they are able to estimate or to evaluate estimated answers. For example, asking students whether "20" is a reasonable answer to the question "What is 10% of the total of 99 + 102?" requires understanding of several computational strategies, which is the curricular goal.

None of the objectives reflected in the other options is as likely to meet the goal. When students use calculators on all mathematical tasks, they may not learn how to estimate or evaluate their answers. Similarly, when they are drilled on number facts, they may not understand the operations they are performing. And while knowing the connections between basic the arithmetic operations is essential, it doesn't necessarily lead to using computational strategies fluently or learning how to estimate appropriately.

Beyond the Question

One way to find relationships within the mathematics curriculum is to have students bring in "real life" uses of mathematics at home (planning time, cooking, budgeting, etc.). What kinds of things could you have children bring from home and how would you relate each to topics in mathematics?

Bring from Home	Mathematics Topics Addressed
_____	_____
_____	_____
_____	_____

Specification 1D | Identify types and uses of curricular materials, media and technologies, and other resources. (For example, in mathematics, measurement equipment, video tapes and disks, computer software, and the Internet.)

About the Specification

Administrators want to hire teachers who are aware of the uses of technology in content areas. In what ways might you use technology in teaching elementary school mathematics?

_____

_____

If you don't know, how might you find out? _____

_____

Students in a fourth-grade class are learning how to copy line segments and angles from their text onto a piece of paper. Which of the following is LEAST likely to help them?

(A) compass

(B) protractor

(C) straight edge

(D) geo-board

About the Question

What do you need to know to be able to answer this question? Do you know what line segments and angles are? If not, where might you learn more?

Do you know what each item listed in the possible answers is? Do you know how to use each? Can you teach their uses to students?

What is the Answer? _____

Explanation of the Answer

It is important for teachers to be familiar with all the various materials, technologies, and resources available to them. As a teacher candidate, you should know how to utilize basic equipment in the classroom. Here you must determine which piece of equipment would "LEAST likely help" fourth-graders in a geometry lesson.

(D) is the correct answer. A geo-board would be least helpful to students copying line segments and angles onto paper. It is used to create figures like rectangles and triangles by stretching rubber bands over a board of evenly spaced nails. The other pieces of equipment are necessary for students to complete the assignment.

TIP: Candidates are encouraged to visit as many classrooms as possible to observe teaching methods and student behavior in action and to see how various curricular materials are put into practice.

Beyond the Question

Look back at the specification. Are you comfortable that you know at least one resource in each of the categories listed? If not, how could you find out what resources exist? (Many administrators say that they ask questions about available mathematics resources when they interview prospective teachers. It will pay for you to have your answers ready.)

Videotapes _____

Videodisks or CDs _____

Computer software _____

Internet resources _____

Other useful resources _____

Mathematics Curriculum Standards

Look back at the student standards for elementary school mathematics for your state. Assuming that you could be hired to teach ANY elementary grade, are there standards that you are NOT sure you could successfully teach? What are they?

Standard	_Grade Level_	_How Can I Learn More?_
_____	_____	_____
_____	_____	_____
_____	_____	_____

INSTRUCTION

Specification 2A Demonstrate knowledge of methods of identifying, assessing, activating, and building on the students' prior knowledge, experiences, cultural backgrounds, and skills in each content area.

About the Specification

Imagine that you are beginning to teach your students the concept of fractions. How might you identify and assess your students' prior knowledge and skills?

_____

_____

One way to introduce fractions to students is to discuss money. How might you discover whether there are cultural differences among your students in their understanding of money?

_____

_____

_____

A culturally diverse fifth-grade class is ready to begin a unit on measurement. The teacher includes in the lesson plan some questions to ask the class before beginning:

● What units of measurement are used to measure length?

● What units of measurement are used to measure weight?

By beginning the unit with these questions for the class, the teacher is most likely doing which of the following?

(A) preparing to teach how to find perimeters

(B) assessing students' prior knowledge

(C) evaluating student's understanding of volume

(D) alerting students that this unit is particularly important

TIP: Don't "overread" a question. Think about exactly what the question is asking—try putting it into your own words—and then select the option that most directly answers the question.

About the Question

What issues of cultural diversity is the teacher likely to find from the answers students give? _____

_____

_____

What is the Answer? _____

Explanation of the Answer

Teachers need to understand their students' current skills and abilities in any area before they can begin to teach them. They have to know what their students know and don't know. They also have to be aware of the backgrounds of their students. Here a teacher is assessing students' understanding by asking questions about measurement. The teacher has to be aware that students may know different systems for measuring length and weight; their answers may include feet, miles, meters, kilometers, pounds, and grams. The teacher has to be able to build on students' varied knowledge when teaching the unit.

(B) is the correct answer. This teacher is assessing students' prior knowledge. Then the teacher may go on to use what he or she has learned to teach such concepts as how to find perimeters or to explain volume, but the first step is finding out what students know.

Beyond the Question

If issues of cultural diversity arise in the class described above, what are some ways the teacher can work with those issues throughout the unit on measurement?

_____

_____

Specification	Demonstrate knowledge of methods of preparing, evaluating, and justifying instructional activities within and across content areas.
2B	

About the Specification

What are the characteristics of effective instructional activities? _____

_____

Think of a mathematics unit you might teach (for example, subtraction of whole numbers). List it here. _____

_____

What are some of the activities you might use with students to teach the elements of subtraction? _____

_____

How would you choose the activities and how would you know if they were successful?

_____

sample question

29
x 57
_____

Before the students in a fifth-grade class solve the problem above, the teacher has them use mental mathematics to compute 9 x 7, 20 x 7, 9 x 50, and 20 x 50. For which of the following reasons would it be appropriate to have the students use mental mathematics in this way?

(A) To show the connection between multiplication and addition

(B) To prepare for an activity involving rounding to the nearest ten

(C) To introduce the associative property of multiplication

(D) To reinforce understanding of a multiplication algorithm

About the Question

What is the connection between multiplication and addition? _____

_____

Why is it useful for students to understand rounding? _____

_____

What is the associative property of multiplication? _____

_____

Why does the multiplication algorithm work the way it does? _____

What is "mental mathematics"? _____

_____

What is the Answer? _____

Explanation of the Answer

Preparing for lessons is as important for students as it is for teachers. Effective teachers assist their students in many kinds of learning activities, especially by building on their prior knowledge and experience. Here a teacher is "pre-teaching" her students by having them use "mental mathematics" to compute multiplication problems that can help them solve the problem that they will then be asked to solve. You are asked why these mental mathematics computations are appropriate.

(D) is the correct answer. Understanding the algorithm involved in multiplication is essential to success in solving multiplication problems. Using mental mathematics is a useful way to comprehend the algorithm.

Beyond the Question

How might you prepare for teaching a unit in mathematics and how might you evaluate your own success?

Choose a topic that you will be required to teach. _____

How would you prepare to teach this unit? _____

_____

How would you evaluate your success? _____

_____

_____

Specification	Select teaching and learning strategies to help individual students or groups of students understand topics and concepts within content areas. (For example, demonstration; cooperative learning; guided oral and silent work; use of journals and logs; graphic organizers; and inquiry method.)
2C	

About the Specification

Imagine that you had a class of second graders who were much stronger in language arts than in mathematics. What kinds of strategies might you use with your class to help them understand addition and subtraction of whole numbers?

_____

_____

sample question

At the beginning of a unit on division, a third-grade teacher asks students working in groups to devise their own methods for dividing 156 gumballs equally among 4 people. The teacher is encouraging the use of all of the following EXCEPT

(A) estimation

(B) guess and check

(C) standard algorithms

(D) cooperative learning

About the Question

How does this question relate to the specification? What strategies is the teacher employing to help students understand the concept of division?

_____

_____

What is the Answer? _____

Explanation of the Answer

Teaching mathematics, like teaching any subject, requires teachers to be able to use strategies that help all of their students understand the material that is being taught. In this scenario, a teacher has students work in groups to come up with their own creative methods of solving a problem. You are asked to identify the one strategy of the four presented that the teacher is NOT encouraging.

(C) is the correct answer. The teacher is NOT encouraging the use of standard algorithms, but is encouraging the use of the other three strategies: estimation, guess and check, and cooperative learning.

Beyond the Question

What activity can you think of to teach a class that dividing a quantity by 1/2 is not the same as dividing that same quantity by 2?

Specification	*Demonstrate knowledge of methods of adjusting instruction to*
2D	*meet students' needs. (For example, corrective and developmental instruction; re-teaching; follow-up and enrichment instruction; and preparation of content area instruction to meet the needs of all readers.)*

About the Specification

Imagine that you have students who don't understand the concept of dividing with remainders, students who have trouble applying what they know about dividing with remainders to "real life" word problems, and students who appear to understand division and remainders completely. How might you adjust your instruction to meet the needs of all of your students?

sample question

When a student does not understand the relationship between decimals and percents after an initial period of instruction, which of the following actions is the most appropriate for the teacher to take?

(A) Assigning homework that will give practice in the application of the concept

(B) Suggesting that the student pay close attention and repeating the explanation more slowly and more clearly

(C) Reviewing the long-division algorithm with the student and focusing on expressing the remainder as a decimal

(D) Re-teaching the concept using examples and/or manipulatives that are different from those used in the initial instruction

About the Question

What is the relationship between decimals and percents? _____

_____

What kinds of "manipulatives" might you use to help students understand this relationship?

_____

What is the Question? _____

Explanation of the Answer

Effective teachers recognize that their students have different learning styles and needs. They know that not all of their students will understand their explanations of new materials, and they are prepared to present materials in a number of ways. Here you see four ways in which a teacher could respond to a student who does not understand the relationship between decimals and percents after it has been explained. You must select the most appropriate of the four possible responses.

(D) is the correct answer. The most appropriate response is to "re-teach" the concept in new ways. In mathematics, it is useful to use different examples and to demonstrate, when possible, using manipulatives that students can see and touch. None of the other responses is appropriate. Option A isn't appropriate because a student can't apply the concept until he or she understands it. Option B is both unhelpful and insensitive to the student. Option C won't help a student who doesn't understand the relationship between decimals and percents.

Beyond the Question

Look at a mathematics book you might actually use in a grade level you hope to teach. List the major mathematics concepts that students are expected to master at that grade level. How would you introduce these concepts to students of varying abilities? Why?

Topic	Ability Level	Introductory Instruction	Rationale
_____	_____	_____	_____
_____	_____	_____	_____
_____	_____	_____	_____
_____	_____	_____	_____

Specification	Demonstrate knowledge of various strategies for motivating students and encouraging their success. (For example, praise, wait time, and token economies.)
2E	

About the Specification

Many students fear and dislike mathematics. What are some ways of helping children develop interest in mathematics and feel successful?

_____

_____

sample question

A fifth-grade teacher is reviewing percents with a class. Which of the following strategies would be the most likely to motivate the students?

(A) Instructing the students to review the basic concepts of percentages in small heterogeneous groups

(B) Assigning a homework sheet that includes various types of problems about percentages

(C) Pretending to be a salesperson in a music store and having the students determine percentage discounts off of their favorite CDs

(D) Re-reading out loud the pages in the textbook that cover percentages and working sample problems on the board

About the Question

Under what circumstances would a teacher review percents with a class?

_____

What are the basic concepts of percents? How would you explain them?

_____

_____

What is the Answer? _____

Explanation of the Answer

Student motivation is a key factor in student success. Teachers play a vital role in providing motivation for students. Here a fifth-grade teacher is reviewing percentages and sees four possible actions to take. You are asked to identify the one that is most likely to motivate the students to learn more about percentages.

(C) is the correct answer. Although each of the four possible actions deals with percentages, the students are much more likely to be motivated by this action. This involves them actively in applying what they know about percentages to a task that is likely to interest them: buying CDs at discount prices.

Beyond the Question

What must the teacher do after conducting the motivating activity? What comes next in this scenario?

_____

What is the relationship between motivating students and their understanding of mathematics?

_____

_____

Specification	Demonstrates knowledge of a variety of approaches to instruction and the theoretical and empirical bases of these approaches. (For example, developmentally appropriate instruction and model-based classroom management.)
2F	

About the Specification

Name three ways of helping elementary students understand area vs. perimeter. On what theories are these approaches based?

Approach	_Theory_
_____	_____
_____	_____
_____	_____

A first grade-teacher, beginning a unit on sets, gave each table of students a collection of buttons and asked the students to put the buttons into groups. They were not given any instructions about grouping them. When all of the students had finished the task at their tables, each group told the rest of the class what characteristics it chose to arrange the buttons. This approach to instruction is best described as

(A) constructivist

(B) coaching

(C) behavioral

(D) modeling

About the Question

In your own words, briefly define the four instructional approaches listed above.

Constructivist _____

Coaching _____

Behavioral _____

Modeling _____

What is the Answer? _____

Explanation of the Answer

Teachers constantly translate theory into practice in the classroom. Their assignments are informed by what they have learned from the work of educational theorists. Here a teacher is introducing a unit on sets by having groups of students sort buttons in whatever ways make the most sense to them; then they explain the reasoning behind their groupings to the rest of the class. You are asked to identify the theoretical approach behind the teacher's assignment.

(A) is the correct answer. The teacher is using a "constructivist" approach" with the class, letting them "construct" their own answers. This allows the teacher both to see how her students are thinking and then to use these thought processes (and concrete examples) to introduce the concept of sets. Although each of the other possible answers is an approach to teaching, none is relevant to this question.

Beyond the Question

How might the teacher begin a unit on sets using a "coaching" approach? In what ways would this be appropriate or inappropriate for this lesson?

_____

_____

How might the teacher begin a unit on sets using a "behavioral" approach? Under what circumstances would this approach be appropriate or inappropriate for this lesson?

_____

_____

Think of a mathematics unit for which a "modeling" approach would be appropriate. What is the unit? Why is modeling the right approach for it?

_____

_____

ASSESSMENT

Specification 3A

Demonstrate knowledge of when and how to use traditional and standardized testing methodologies. (For example, standardized tests, publisher-produced tests, screening tests.)

About the Specification

Of what use are standardized tests in mathematics for elementary students? Who should receive the data about the results? Why?

Uses of standardized tests: _____

Who should receive data?	_Why?_
_____	_____
_____	_____
_____	_____
_____	_____

sample question

In presenting standardized achievement test results to a student's parents, a teacher explains that the student's stanine score of 7 on the mathematics sub-test indicates performance that is

(A) substantially below average

(B) somewhat below average

(C) average

(D) somewhat above average

About the Question

Before looking at the explanation of the answer below, explain here what a "stanine" is and what a "stanine score" means.

_____

_____

What is the Answer? _____

Explanation of the Answer

Teachers are not only expected to understand how to use traditional and standardized testing methodologies, but they are also expected to be able to explain them to parents. In this question a teacher explains to parents what a stanine score of 7 indicates.

(D) is the correct answer. Stanines divide a score scale into nine parts, with fixed percentages of students falling into each stanine. Dividing scores into stanines is a way of creating a "bell curve" and describing where a test-taker's score falls within that bell-shaped curve. From stanines 1 to 5, the percentages are 4, 7, 12, 17, and 20, respectively. From stanines 6 to 9, the percentages are 17, 12, 7, and 4, respectively. Stanines 1, 2, and 3 are considered below average. Stanines 4, 5, and 6 are considered average, and stanines 7, 8, and 9 are considered above average. A score of 7 is somewhat above average.

Beyond the Question

When and why is it useful for scores to be reported in stanines?

_____

Imagine that you have a student whose mathematics score falls into the fourth stanine. The child's parents want to know what stanines are and what the "fourth stanine" means. Put into your own words what you would say to the parents (and assume that they have no knowledge of testing or the reporting of test scores).

_____

_____

Specification

3B

Demonstrate knowledge of various classroom-based, informal, or nontraditional assessment strategies. (For example, observation; portfolios; and performance samples).

About the Specification

When might each of these approaches be used to assess elementary students' mathematics skills?

Observation: _____

Portfolios: _____

Performance samples: _____

Other approaches: _____

sample question

As part of a concrete introduction to basic algebraic equations, students have been learning to use a scale balance to weigh various objects. Which of the following strategies would best help the teacher assess students' skills with this piece of equipment?

(A) performance sample

(B) written test

(C) portfolio

(D) small group observation

About the Question

How would learning to use a scale balance help students understand algebraic equations?

_____

_____

What is the Answer? _____

Explanation of the Answer

It is just as important for a teacher to be able to match the appropriate assessment strategy with the material being taught as it is to teach the lessons. In this example, you are to choose the strategy that would BEST help a teacher assess students who have learned to use a scale balance.

(A) is the correct answer. A scale balance is a piece of equipment that needs to be used correctly in order to balance various materials. Students can best show that they have learned the necessary skill by individually "performing" in front of the teacher. The other strategies are not as appropriate because they do not include individual hands-on interaction with the balance. Thus, although the students might be able to describe the use of the balance, the teacher won't know whether they can actually use the equipment without seeing them use it.

Beyond the Question

What are the best uses of informal assessment in elementary mathematics?

_____

What are the best uses of formal assessments?

_____

How can the two types of assessment work be used together to help teachers assess students?

_____

Specification	Interpret data obtained from various formal and informal assessments.
3C	

About the Specification

Assessment in education means collecting information. Teachers use the information to see whether their students have learned the concepts that they have been taught. The purpose of assessment is not to "grade" students on their knowledge. Assessment is essential to inform teachers about their own success—and to help them see what they need to teach again for students who didn't fully understand the material the first time it was presented.

What are other purposes of assessment, both formal and informal?

_____

_____

sample question

A mathematics teacher determines that the median score by her students on a test about fractions is 87 percent. The results specifically tell which of the following?

(A) 87 percent is the most common score on the test

(B) 87 percent is the arithmetic average of the test

(C) Half of the students scored below 87 percent, while half score above 87 percent

(D) The highest score obtained by the students is 87 percent

About the Question

Before you look at the explanation of the answer, explain the following in your own words:

Mode _____

Mean _____

Median _____

Maximum _____

What is the Answer? _____

Explanation of the Answer

Teachers often need to interpret data from assessments that they have created or that came from other sources. This can assist them in having a better understanding of which skills individuals or classes have learned and which need to be re-taught. In this question, you are to identify the meaning of a median score of 87 percent.

(A) "The most common score" is the MODE.

(B) "The arithmetic average" is the MEAN.

(C) is the correct answer. A particular "median score" means that one-half of the students performed below that score and one-half performed above.

(D) "The highest score" is the MAXIMUM.

TIP: As a teacher candidate, you should be familiar with basic statistical terminology such as mean, median, mode, range, maximum, and minimum. How are they calculated? What do they tell you? What can you learn from them?

In this example, the teacher might be pleased to find that more than half the class scored 87 or above, but might want to look closely at the scores of students who fell below the median, examine how far below the median they fell, and then study their answer patterns to see if they made similar mistakes, which might suggest areas that need some re-teaching. Remember that testing is not an isolated activity. Teachers use tests to gain insight into what their students know and don't know and they use the results of assessments to inform their teaching.

Beyond the Question

The most important thing about all of these terms is knowing what they represent—and knowing that when people use data, they have selected one of these representations. For example, if a group of your students scored 46, 46, 46, 78, 80, 90, and 100 (on a test with 100 possible points), which method of reporting scores would make these look the best (besides "maximum")? Which method would make them look the worst?

Best _____ Worst _____

What if the students' scores were 0, 10, 22, 25, 45, 88, 88? Which method would make them look the best? Which would make them look the worst?

Best _____ Worst _____

Specification	Identify common points of confusion or misconception among
3D	elementary school learners in the various content areas. (For example, errors and patterns of error; inaccurate factual knowledge, misconceptions about processes or relationships; "buggy" algorithms.)

About the Specification

What are some of the most common misconceptions and mistakes you are likely to find as a teacher of elementary mathematics?

_____

_____

Of these, which do feel you cannot teach well? Where do you need to "brush up" before you begin teaching?

_____

_____

$^4/_{16} - ^1/_8 = ^3/_8$

$^5/_9 - ^1/_2 = ^4/_7$

$^7/_{16} - ^1/_5 = ^6/_{11}$

The examples above are representative of a student's work. If the error pattern indicated in these examples continues, the student's answer to the problem $^9/_{11} - ^1/_7$ is most likely to be:

(A) $^{10}/_4$

(B) $^8/_7$

(C) $^8/_4$

(D) $^9/_8$

About the Question

What is the student doing wrong? _____

_____

What does the student NOT understand? _____

_____

What is the Answer? _____

Explanation of the Answer

Patterns of errors can often reveal common points of confusion or misconception by students. The example here is revealing for the teacher, who can see where this student is going wrong in subtracting fractions. This is a very common problem for students who are beginning to subtract fractions. It shows that a student really doesn't understand what the numbers represent, or what the operation means.

(C) is the correct answer. This student is subtracting numerators, then subtracting denominators, and putting one on top of the other to form the fraction that appears as the "answer." The student doesn't understand that the fractions must be made to be equivalent before subtraction can take place.

In the next problem you can see by the error pattern that the student would subtract 1 from 9 and 7 from 11, resulting in an answer of 8/4. This is not a correct subtracting of fractions, but it is the correct answer to this question.

Beyond the Question

The student's problem is an example of a "buggy algorithm," which is a flawed understanding of a process or concept. What other specific "buggy algorithms" can you expect to encounter with elementary mathematics students? How can you assess to find out if your students have these problems?

"Buggy Algorithm"   *Possible Assessment*

_____   _____

_____   _____

_____   _____

PUTTING IT ALL TOGETHER

MATHEMATICS

Now that you have worked through this section of the workbook, you should have a general idea of what curriculum, instruction, and assessment issues are likely to appear on the test. The following chart is intended to help you think about the areas in which you might need further review before you take the test.

In addition, here is a list of topics that might appear on the test in the context of curriculum, instruction, and assessment in this subject area. Can you answer questions on these topics?

Sample Topics

- Pre-number concepts, decimal numeration, operations on sets of numbers
- Geometry: non-metric, metric, and coordinate
- Number theory
- Problem-solving
- Estimation and approximation
- Probability and statistics
- Hand-held calculators and computers
- Use of manipulatives and other appropriate materials
- Analysis of students' work in mathematics
- Content-specific pedagogy

If you are working in a study group, you might try asking each other questions on these topics. You might also challenge each other to come up with questions based on the topics and on the specifications that appear throughout this section.

STUDY PLAN: MATHEMATICS

Content areas I need to study	Materials I have	Materials I need	Where can I find material I need?

SCIENCE | *Curriculum, Instruction, Assessment*

Specification **1A**	*Identify broad purposes for teaching all content areas and identify purposes for teaching particular topics within each content area. (For example: developing orderly processes of thought in science).*

About the Specification

Look at your state standards for elementary science. What are some of the general knowledge and skills that children are expected to develop in elementary school? _____

_____

Do the knowledge and skills change over the years in elementary school or do they build on each other from one year to the next? For example: is the first-grade science curriculum related to the fourth-grade science curriculum? If so, how are they related?

_____

_____

sample question

The table and graph below were produced by a group of students during an activity designed to help them collect and graph data and organize information.

Which feedback from the teacher would best facilitate student understanding?

(A) Students should always use units when measuring variables.

(B) Students should produce a data table to organize their information.

(C) Students should keep the intervals of each axis consistent.

(D) Students should use an appropriate title when producing their graph.

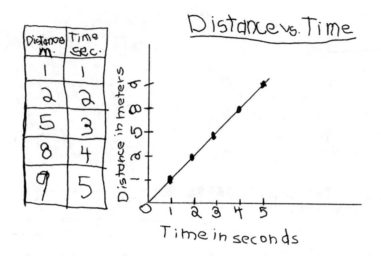

Distance vs. Time

Time in seconds

About the Question

Why is it important for students to make tables and graphs as a science activity?

What is the Answer? _____

Explanation of the Question

Presenting information graphically is a common goal of most science curricula. Involving students in creating their own graphs further encourages their learning.

In this question, students have produced both a table and a graph, but the information they present is not presented accurately and their graphic representation does not match the data in their table. In answering this question, you might picture yourself as the teacher who explains what went wrong between the data table and the graph.

(A) The students did use units of measure in their work, so this is not useful feedback for them.

(B) The students did produce a data table, so this suggestion is not helpful.

(C) is the correct answer. The students' data table results are not accurately plotted on their graph because they did not keep the intervals consistent on their vertical axis ("distance in meters"). To facilitate their understanding, the teacher should explain (and demonstrate) how to use units of measure consistently on a graph.

(D) The graph does have an appropriate title ("Distance vs. Time") so this feedback is not appropriate.

Beyond the Question

Think about a grade level you would like to teach. Think of one science content area you would be required to teach at that grade level. What units would you teach to help your students understand that science content area?

Specification

1B | Understand the relationship of subject area "parts" to subject area "wholes" for instructional planning and the instructional implications of these relationships.

About the Specification

Look at a current textbook or curriculum that you might be asked to use in an elementary science classroom. Is it arranged according to "wholes" and "parts" (such as "concepts" and "units")? If so, what are they and how are they related?

	Concepts	*Units*	*Relationships*
1.	_____	_____	_____
2.	_____	_____	_____
3.	_____	_____	_____

sample question

The following is an excerpt from a whole scope and sequence for a second-grade science class.

> The teacher will open various sealed containers one at a time. Each container will hold one of the following: chocolate, bananas, perfume, soup, oranges, soap, vinegar, and strawberries. The teacher will ask students to raise their hands as soon as they are able to smell the substance. Discussion will take place as to the reason why students closest to the opened container usually noticed the odor first.

The activity above can best be integrated into which of the following modules from a science textbook?

(A) Life Science: Classifying Living Things

(B) Physical Science: Properties of Matter

(C) Earth Science: Weather and Climate

(D) Environmental Science: Endangered Plant Species

About the Question

What can happen in a science classroom if the teacher doesn't understand the parts that make up the whole subject area? _____

What is the Answer? _____

Explanation of the Answer

Teachers serve as "guides" for students, leading them to discovery and learning. Effective teachers are able to guide students from the specific findings of a "hands on" experiment to the broader principles and theories behind the experimental results. In the example included in this question, the teacher is doing exactly that—assisting students in understanding the relationship between their own sensory experience and the scientific principles that explain their experience.

You are asked to decide which science module is being demonstrated by this experiment.

(B) is the correct answer. This is an experiment that would fit into a science textbook under the heading "Physical Science: Properties of Matter." None of the other possible answers correctly identifies the field of science that the demonstration addresses.

Beyond the Question

Notice that the teacher demonstrates not only an understanding of the relationship between the <u>content</u> "whole" and "part," but also between the <u>activity</u> as a part of a larger learning process. Parts and wholes, then, involve knowing what sub-areas to teach, and how to make the specific activities relate to the larger "wholes" being learned.

There is increasing pressure for elementary teachers to be good teachers of science. Looking back at the science text you have examined, are there content area "wholes" you think you need to understand more thoroughly before you begin to teach? If so, where can you find the information you need?

I would like to know more about _____

I can try these sources for information _____

Specification 1C | *Understand relationships among concepts both within and across content areas and the instructional implications of these interrelationships. (For example: use of estimation in a variety of problem solving situations in different disciplines.)*

About the Specification

Given what you are learning about your state standards in areas other than science, think about some concepts that could apply to language arts and science, mathematics and science, or social studies and science. Knowledge of these relationships will be fruitful in designing activities for your students.

Science and Language Arts   *Science and Mathematics*   *Science and Social Studies*

_____   _____   _____

_____   _____   _____

_____   _____   _____

sample question

Students hung four different cast iron masses on the spring shown below, recorded the distance that the spring was stretched by each mass, and recorded the four measurements in the table below. Next the teacher asked the students to use the table to determine the distance that the spring would be stretched by a mass of 150 grams.

The experiment and the problem posed would be most appropriate in helping the students explore which of the following key concepts of mathematics?

(A) Decimals

(B) Average

(C) Proportion

(D) Percent

Mass (in g.)	Distance Stretched (in cm.)
40	2.0
50	2.5
80	4.0
100	5.0
150	- - -

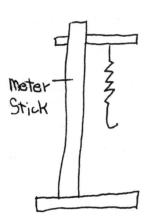

Meter Stick

About the Question

The concepts of "proportion" and "percent" range across many disciplines and it is essential that students understand them. However, students are frequently confused about the differences between the two. Can you clearly describe both concepts?

Proportion is _____

Percent is _____

What is the Answer? _____

Explanation of the Answer

Teachers must be able to understand, explain, and demonstrate how concepts can be utilized across disciplines. In the scenario presented here, the teacher is relating mathematics and science. You must identify which mathematical concept is being used and therefore, what kind of mathematics preparation would be most helpful for students.

(A) "Decimals" are an important part of the study of mathematics, but they are not the key concept here.

(B) "Average" is a also an important concept but it is not involved in this experiment.

(C) is the correct answer. Proportion is the key mathematical concept that the teacher is presenting, and it is therefore the most appropriate to teach in relation to the experiment.

(D) "Percent" is a kind of proportion, but it is not the kind of proportion that is being presented here.

Beyond the Question

Look back at some of the topics you wrote down under specification IC for science (see above). Given the grade levels noted below, think of an activity that might link topics for students.

1st grade language arts and science: _____

_____

3rd grade science and mathematics: _____

_____

5th grade science and social studies: _____

_____

Linking topics across content areas makes learning interesting, relevant, and memorable for students.

Specification	Identify types and uses of curricular materials, media and technologies, and other resources. (For example: books, software, equipment, materials, and displays in science.)
1D	

About the Specification

If you were hired to teach elementary school near your home, what materials would you use to teach science? Have you seen and used those materials?

Choose a grade level that interests you and find out what science materials are used at that level. If you can, visit an elementary school and see the materials for yourself.

Grade Level: _____

Books: _____

Equipment: _____

Materials: _____

Many districts require that new teachers be aware of software for teaching children. What do you know about available software (and Internet resources) for teaching science at a grade level that interests you? If you don't know about available software, how would you find out?

Software: _____

Ways of locating useful software: _____

sample question

Literature can be a valuable way to introduce a science unit. Here an early elementary teacher uses a picture book about clouds in a unit on weather. The teacher is most likely to use such a book in a science unit for second or third graders to:

(A) Illustrate a process of scientific inquiry for students to use in experiments

(B) Involve the students in using their imaginations in thinking about the sky

(C) Provide a list of facts about clouds for the students to memorize

(D) Present the students with factual information on which they will be tested later

About the Question

The National Standards for Student Learning in Science require that students understand scientific inquiry. What is scientific inquiry? _____

➡ Explanation of the Answer

Teachers should be able to use a variety of curricular materials in their teaching. In this example, a second or third grade teacher is planning to use a picture book about clouds in teaching a unit on weather. You are asked to identify the reason that would lead an early elementary teacher to use such a children's book in a science lesson.

(B) is the correct answer. It is most likely that the teacher has selected this book to stimulate students to use their imaginations in thinking about the sky. It is not likely that the teacher is providing facts for the students, nor is it likely that the teacher expects students of this age to understand the process of scientific inquiry.

Beyond the Question

What other materials might you use to introduce second graders to a unit on weather? _____

_____

INSTRUCTION

Specification 2A	Demonstrate knowledge of methods of identifying, assessing, activating, and building on the students' prior knowledge, experiences, cultural backgrounds, and skills in each content area.

About the Specification

Science is a content area in which prior knowledge and skills must exist before new learning can take place. Constantly checking and building on students' knowledge and skills will help ensure that students will leave elementary school possessing the necessary understanding of science fundamentals to be successful in secondary school.

Think of a unit you might be called upon to teach in science (for example, a second-grade unit on ecological systems or on trash management).

Science unit I might teach: _____

What prior knowledge and skills must students possess to learn this unit?

_____

_____

How will you find out whether or not the students possess the necessary knowledge and skills to begin the new unit?

_____

_____

sample question

Students in a science class have been learning how to separate various mixtures into individual components. Which of the following is the best instructional method to identify a student's acquired skills in this area?

(A) Have the student separate a few mixtures and solutions while the teacher observes.

(B) Have the student write an essay about the proper method to separate a few mixtures and solutions.

(C) Have the student work with a small group whose objective is to separate a few mixtures and solutions.

(D) Have the student describe for the teacher how to separate a few mixtures and solutions.

About the Question

Which part of the specification covers this question? _____

What is the Answer? _____

Explanation of the Answer

Teachers often need to identify and assess their students' acquisitions of skills in a content area. In this example, students have been learning how to separate mixtures and solutions. You are asked to determine the BEST instructional method a teacher might use to identify a student's skills in this area.

(A) is the correct answer. Having the individual student perform the required task is often the best way to identify and assess skills. It can be time consuming, but it can also be the best method of assessment.

(B) Writing about a task is not the same as performing it, especially when the task specifically requires the use of dexterity, measurement, and scientific instruments.

(C) Many times it is difficult to identify a particular student's skills when working in a group, because other students often do more or less than their share.

(D) As in (A), re-telling is not the same as performing.

Beyond the Question

Imagine that it is the beginning of the year at the next grade level and you need to know whether your students know how to separate various mixtures into individual components before you can begin science instruction. How would you assess their prior skill?

_____

_____

Specification	Demonstrate knowledge of methods of preparing, evaluating,
2B	and justifying instructional activities within and across content areas.

About the Specification

Instructional activities must be appropriate for student learning as well as for educational goals. What kinds of instructional activities might be appropriate for teaching lower-elementary students about genetics?

Learning Goal

Activity

[Example] Introduction to Genetics

Have students look at eye and hair colors of their family members and draw conclusions

_____   _____

_____   _____

_____   _____

_____   _____

                               _____

While learning about plants, students in a particular classroom were engaged in a variety of activities related to the topic. Some created a mural; several wrote and acted out a short play; others observed and recorded plant growth; several composed and sang a song about the development of plants; another group worked with the teacher in the reading center, discussing a chapter on plants from the science textbook; others worked alone, reading non-fiction books on plants. The teacher was most likely providing a variety of activities to

(A) recognize the different learning styles of the students

(B) allow students to move around the classroom

(C) provide opportunities for students to engage in artistic activities

(D) instruct students in ways of collecting accurate data about plants

About the Question

How is this question related to the specification? _____

What is the Answer? _____

Explanation of the Answer

(A) is the correct answer. The teacher is most likely recognizing the different learning styles of the students. By doing so, the teacher is also increasing the opportunities for learning in the classroom.

(B) Allowing students to move around the classroom is not an instructional technique in itself, and it is only a small part of what is taking place in the classroom that is described here.

(C) Providing opportunities for students to engage in artistic activities is useful in some teaching and learning situations, but it is only one activity of the many going on in the classroom described in this scenario.

(D) Some of the students in this class are learning about collecting accurate data about plants, but this is not a comprehensive view of the classroom nor is it the only goal of the teacher.

Beyond the Question

What has to happen in the classroom besides the activities themselves in order for learning to take place? _____

What methods would you recommend to the teacher for follow-up to the activities listed above?_____

_____

| **Specification** **2C** | *Select teaching and learning strategies to help individual students or groups of students understand topics and concepts within content areas. (For example: demonstration; cooperative learning; guided oral and silent work; use of journals and logs; graphic organizers; and inquiry method.)* |

About the Specification

When is demonstration useful for science instruction? _____

_____

When is cooperative learning useful for science instruction? _____

_____

What are some ways that journals can help students learn science? _____

_____

What is "inquiry method" as it relates to science? _____

_____

What are some ways of teaching the inquiry method to elementary students? _____

_____

sample question

A science teacher plans to teach a health education unit on nutrition. Students are divided into heterogeneous groups of four members. Each group is assigned a different section of the same article to read, to summarize, and to become ready to teach to fellow students. Students then regroup, with members of the new groups representing all four sections. Each member of the new groups teaches the other three group members about his or her section of the article. Which of the following teaching and learning strategies is best described by this exercise?

(A) demonstration

(B) portfolio

(C) jigsaw method

(D) think-pair-share

What is the "jigsaw method"? _____

_____

What is the purpose of the "jigsaw method"? _____

_____

What is "think-pair-share"? _____

_____

What is the purpose of "think-pair-share"? _____

_____

What is the Answer? _____

Explanation of the Answer

Selecting appropriate teaching strategies is an important ingredient in a teacher's overall effectiveness in helping students learn. One of the primary goals of instruction is to keep students involved in their own education by having them be responsible as a group or as individuals for their learning. Here students are working in groups and will read and discuss a specific part of an article on nutrition, knowing that they will be responsible for teaching other students about their parts. You are asked to identify the teaching and learning strategy described by this assignment.

(C) is the correct answer. The jigsaw method is being described here. Its premise is to break material down into smaller units, thereby allowing for more in-depth analysis, discussion, and teaching. Students will "assemble" the sections of the article into a whole as they are taught about each section by their fellow students.

Beyond the Question

In a sentence, summarize the differences between "think-pair-share" and the "jigsaw method." _____

_____

Is there a difference in purpose between the two methods? In other words, is one better than the other for accomplishing specific goals? If so, which goals are likely to be met by each method? _____

_____

_____

_____

Name one possible problem with the activity described in the question. _____

_____

What would you recommend the teacher do as a follow-up to the activity described
above?_____

Specification	Demonstrate knowledge of methods of adjusting instruction to meet students' needs. (For example: corrective and developmental instruction; re-teaching; follow-up and enrichment instruction; and preparation of content area instruction to meet the needs of all students.)
2D	

About the Specification

Science methods often need re-teaching and follow-up instruction. As a result, teachers need to have "back-up plans" that involve new ways of explaining the material they teach.

As a teacher, what would you do if your students didn't seem to understand the point of an experiment they had just conducted? For example: you have completed an experiment on plants' absorption of colored light, but your students don't seem to "get it." What would you do?_____

_____

_____

_____

sample question

A class is about to participate in a hands-on science experiment. One student uses a wheelchair and cannot reach the table where the lab has been set up. What would be the most effective course of action for the teacher to take to ensure this student's full participation?

(A) Give the physically challenged student a worksheet that covers the same information the rest of the class is learning.

(B) Place the physically challenged student in a location that makes it easy to observe the experiment from a wheelchair.

(C) Set up an additional lab area in the classroom that is within reach of the physically challenged student.

(D) Send the physically challenged student to another classroom until the experiment is completed.

About the Question

What is the teacher's learning goal for the student in the wheelchair? Is this learning goal the same or different for the rest of the students in the class?

_____

_____

What is it, then, that the teacher must accomplish for the student in the wheelchair?

_____

What is the Answer? _____

Explanation of the Answer

Teachers should be able to adjust their instructional methods to meet the special needs of their students. In this question, you are asked to identify the most effective course of action to take with a student who cannot reach the lab table because the student uses a wheelchair.

(A) is not an effective action. Students in wheelchairs need to be provided with the same opportunities for "hands-on" learning as all other students. Giving a worksheet to this student is not an appropriate alternative to participating in a science experiment.

(B) is not an effective action. Observing other students is not the same as participating and is not likely to yield comparable learning outcomes.

(C) is the correct answer. Setting up an additional lab area in the classroom that is within reach of the student in a wheelchair is an effective course of action. Additionally, if the experiment is to be performed by groups of students, the physically challenged student should be included in a group and all members of the group should work in the wheelchair-accessible lab area.

(D) is not an effective action. Sending the physically challenged student to another classroom until the experiment is completed is unwarranted and counterproductive. The goal of the science teacher in this case is to involve ALL students in the experience and in the learning that results from hands-on experimentation.

Beyond the Question

As a teacher, what questions do you need to ask yourself to ensure that your instruction is appropriate for ALL students in your classes?

_____

_____

_____

Specification	Demonstrate knowledge of various strategies for motivating
2E	*students and encouraging their success. (For example: praise,*
	wait time, and token economies.)

About the Specification

Many students are easily discouraged in learning about science. Some have heard that science is really important and have inferred that it is complex and difficult. Others have trouble learning to "think scientifically." What kinds of things might you do as a teacher to encourage the success of your students who are studying science?

_____

_____

Obviously, you would like students to be interested in learning about science. What other qualities would you like to help instill in your students as you teach science?

_____

_____

sample question

An elementary teacher offers tokens and stickers as rewards for students who can explain the health consequences of smoking cigarettes. This strategy is an example of

(A) intrinsic motivation

(B) extrinsic motivation

(C) negative reinforcement

(D) continuous reinforcement

About the Specification

What is the purpose of offering tokens and stickers as rewards? _____

_____

What is the Answer? _____

80 / Science

Explanation of the Answer

Teachers must understand and be able to apply a variety of strategies for motivating students. As a test-taker, you will be expected to be able to identify motivational strategies by name and to apply them to specific cases.

Here you are asked to identify which type of strategy is being utilized by the teacher who offers tokens and stickers as rewards for learning.

(A) "Intrinsic motivation" comes from INSIDE the student. A student who says, for example, "I want to learn everything there is to know about dinosaurs" is probably intrinsically motivated.

(B) is the correct answer. "Extrinsic motivation" comes from OUTSIDE the student. Offering rewards of any kind to students—whether they are tokens, stickers, candy, or a longer "recess" period—provides extrinsic motivation.

(C) "Negative reinforcement" refers to discouraging or punishing behaviors that teachers deem inappropriate. For example: a child who is talking with nearby students instead of reading might be sent to an isolated desk in the back of the room. This would "negatively reinforce" talking at inappropriate times.

(D) "Continuous reinforcement" refers to constant affirmation of students. Teachers who use "brainstorming," for instance, often use a simple technique of continuous reinforcement. They ask students for suggestions and write every one on a chalkboard, saying something like "good suggestion" or "yes, that's a good one," each time a suggestion is offered. This continuous reinforcement creates a classroom climate in which all of the students are encouraged to participate.

Beyond the Question

What is one way of <u>intrinsically</u> motivating students to understand the health consequences of smoking cigarettes? _____

_____

What is the danger of using only <u>extrinsic</u> motivation with students? _____

_____

Specification	Demonstrates knowledge of a variety of approaches to instruction and the theoretical and empirical bases of these approaches. (For example: developmentally appropriate instruction and model-based classroom management.)
2F	

About the Specification

Science teaching lends itself to many approaches for both lower-elementary and upper-elementary students. Suppose you wanted to introduce lower-elementary students to the inquiry method. What activities might you employ?

What activities might you employ with upper-elementary students?

_____

_____

sample question

A highly visual learner is most likely to learn the key concepts in a chapter on the human skeletal system by doing which of the following?

(A) taking careful notes when the teacher reviews the chapter

(B) re-reading the chapter at home with more privacy

(C) discussing the key concepts with fellow students in a small group

(D) drawing a web diagram of the key concepts presented in the chapter

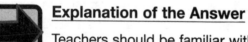

About the Question

Which theorist is associated with the term "visual learner"? _____

What other types of learners does this theorist identify? _____

_____

What is the Answer? _____

Explanation of the Answer

Teachers should be familiar with several methods of instruction, as well as the theories behind those methods, in order to adapt their teaching to meet a variety of learning styles present in a classroom of students. In this question, you are to identify how a "highly visual learner" might BEST learn the key concepts of the human skeletal system.

(A) Note-taking involves groups of words on a page, and this is often confusing to the visual learner.

(B) Re-reading words does not help these learners because, as in (A), it fails to organize the material in a visual manner.

(C) Verbalizing the concepts has the same drawbacks as (A) and (B).

(D) is the correct answer. Graphic organizers, web diagrams, and illustrations all help visual learners, because they organize the material to be learned using a format that is easily accessible to these students. This is a finding of Howard Gardner's work on "multiple intelligences."

Beyond the Question

How might other types of learners best learn key concepts about the human skeletal system?

Type of Learner	_Activity_
_____	_____
_____	_____
_____	_____
_____	_____
_____	_____
_____	_____

ASSESSMENT

Specification 3A — _Demonstrate knowledge of when and how to use traditional and standardized testing methodologies. (For example: standardized tests, publisher-produced tests, screening tests.)_

About the Specification

What kinds of standardized tests are students usually required to take in your state?

_____

When are they required to take them? _____

What do the tests assess? _____

If you haven't seen samples of the tests, how might you see them? _____

_____

It's important for teachers to know as much as possible about the tests their students will be taking. If you are not already familiar with the tests your state requires, you should review them before you begin to teach.

In an upper elementary class, which of the following assessment tools would most effectively determine the ability of each student to explain the differences between mass and volume?

(A) a true-or-false test

(B) a multiple-choice test

(C) an essay test

(D) a small-group performance test

About the Question

Each type of test listed above has its place in assessing student learning. What are some ways that you might use each type to assess learning in science? (Give examples.)

True-or-false test: _____

Multiple-choice test: _____

Essay test: _____

Small-group performance test: _____

What is the Answer? _____

Explanation of the Answer

Assessment is a critical part of successful teaching. Effective teachers know how to use both formal and informal tests and other evaluative instruments to determine what their students have learned and what they have not yet mastered.

This question inquires about the most effective testing method to determine a student's ability to explain the differences between mass and volume. They key words here are "each student" and "explain." When you look at the possible answers, ask yourself which one offers the teacher the best opportunity to assess the level of understanding of each student in the class AND which offers individual students the best opportunity for explaining.

(A) A true-or-false test offers no opportunity for explanation.

(B) A multiple-choice test also offers no opportunity for explanation.

(C) is the correct answer. An essay test (also called a "constructed-response" test) offers the best opportunity for explanation. In an essay test, students are given a question and asked to "construct" their own written response. This type of test would offer students the best opportunity to explain their understanding of the differences between mass and volume.

(D) A small-group performance test does not allow the teacher to readily assess the skills of individual students, and the emphasis is on "doing" rather than "explaining."

Beyond the Question

Teachers must understand what information each type of test is most likely to yield and they must be able to select the test that meets their assessment needs. Teachers are often required by their school, district, or state to give standardized tests to students. Usually, they receive reports on the performance of their students or classes on these standardized tests. How can teachers productively use the information that these reports provide?

Specification	Demonstrate knowledge of various classroom-based, informal, or nontraditional assessment strategies. (For example: observation; oral reports; running records; portfolios; and performance samples).
3B	

About the Specification

What is an example of "informal assessment" in an elementary science class?

Would you choose to use any of the assessment strategies listed in parentheses in the specification above in teaching science? If so, which strategies would you use—and for what purposes?

Assessment Strategy   *Purpose*

_____   _____

_____   _____

_____   _____

sample question

While the teacher observes, a student in an upper elementary science class conducts an experiment. The student weighs dry chemicals on a scale, mixes them together with water, and tests the solution for acidity, using litmus paper.

The activity above can be categorized as which of the following?

(A) portfolio assessment

(B) performance assessment

(C) written assessment

(D) student self-assessment

About the Question

There is a big difference between being able to <u>do</u> a science experiment and being able to <u>explain</u> the results of an experiment. As a result, each requires a different kind of assessment technique.

In what ways might a teacher assess a student's ability to <u>do</u> a science experiment?

_____

In what ways might a teacher assess a student's ability to <u>explain</u> the results of a science experiment?

_____

What is the Answer? _____

Explanation of the Answer

Successful teachers know how to match the proper assessment strategy with the material being taught. It is important to be familiar with several formal and informal methods of assessment. In this question, a student is weighing, mixing, and testing chemicals while the teacher observes. You are to identify which type of assessment is being used.

(B) is the correct answer. The student is "performing" for the teacher. The goal of this performance is to demonstrate acquired skills and knowledge. The other choices are valid types of assessment but are not correct answers to this question.

TIP: There is often a key word that will help you answer a question, especially those whose answer choices are short. Here, the key word is "performance," and even if you are not familiar with the particular type of assessment, you can determine that it is correct from the context of the question: here the students are "performing" for the teacher.

Beyond the Question

How might a teacher conduct a portfolio assessment in science?

_____

What are some types of portfolio assessment? What is the purpose of each?

Portfolio Type	_Purpose_
_____	_____
_____	_____
_____	_____

| Specification | Interpret data obtained from various formal and informal |
| 3C | assessments. |

About the Specification

When teachers give tests, what they get back is "data" on student performance (i.e., how well students have learned the material the test assesses). This data is interpreted by teachers and used to inform their subsequent instructional decisions. "Data" is another word for "information." Assessment, then, is a kind of information gathering. Various types of assessments will provide various kinds of information.

What kinds of information does a teacher receive from a multiple-choice, end-of-unit test created by the publisher of science textbook? _____

_____

What kinds of information does a teacher receive from a cumulative portfolio of a student's work in science over the course of a semester?_____

_____

sample question

A third-grade class has just completed a science unit on the solar system. After giving the students a blank "map" of the solar system and asking them to fill in the names of the planets in their correct locations, the teacher finds that 86% of the class fails to locate the planets correctly.

Which of the following teacher responses would be the most appropriate?

(A) Move on to the next unit because this particular concept is difficult for third-graders.

(B) Move on to the next unit because this concept will be taught again in fifth grade.

(C) Re-teach the concept by making an overhead projection of the correct planetary order for the students to copy onto paper.

(D) Re-teach the concept by having each student draw a representation of the solar system, label each planet, and color each.

About the Question

A goal of assessment should be to determine what has been mastered and what needs to be re-taught. The point of testing is to find out what students have learned and what they have not yet learned. The goal is to re-teach the material they haven't learned yet, in a way that will be more likely to result in mastery.

What other activities might this teacher design to re-teach the order of the planets in the solar system? _____

_____

What is the Answer? _____

Explanation of the Answer

One of the more difficult tasks confronting teachers is to decide what to do if a significant number of students perform poorly on an assessment. Time constraints, including curriculum coverage, standardized testing deadlines, and lesson planning, all add to this difficulty. Here you are to determine the MOST appropriate response if a large percentage of your class failed a particular assessment.

(A) This is often an "easy out" for teachers but is rarely the correct response, because it sells short both their teaching ability and their students' capacity to learn. In this case, third-graders should be able to identify the order of the planets.

(B) This is similar to (A) because it offers a "rationalization" to move on.

(C) Re-teaching is often the best response, but it requires employing a new instructional method to present the material. This option is not the best choice because it only involves copying from an overhead and doesn't require students to engage with the subject in a meaningful way.

(D) is the correct answer. More students are likely to learn the order of the planets if they draw their own "solar system" and label the planets correctly. This method of re-teaching engages the students' visual, artistic, and linguistic abilities and gives them "ownership" of the task.

Beyond the Question

Are there any kinds of assessment data that you are not comfortable interpreting or that seem unclear to you? Now is the time to learn to interpret data from all types of tests. You will need to understand test results to inform your teaching (and re-teaching), to provide feedback to students, and to inform parents when necessary. List below the types of assessment data about which you need more information.

Types of Data	_Types of Tests_	_Sources of Information_
_____	_____	_____
_____	_____	_____
_____	_____	_____
_____	_____	_____
_____	_____	_____

<table>
<tr><td></td><td>**Specification**

3D</td><td>*Identify common points of confusion or misconception among elementary school learners in the various content areas. (For example, errors and patterns of error; inaccurate factual knowledge or vocabulary; misconceptions about processes or relationships.)*</td></tr>
</table>

About the Specification

There may be more misconceptions in elementary science than in any other subject. Research has shown that students' misconceptions, unless discovered and corrected, persist into adulthood. In fact, it is the elementary-level misconceptions about science that lead to many of the problems experienced by science students in college.

What common misconceptions do you know that <u>early-elementary</u> learners are likely to have about science concepts and terms?

_____

_____

What common misconceptions do you know that <u>upper-elementary</u> learners are likely to have about science concepts and terms?

_____

_____

sample question

Whenever children are encouraged to investigate scientific concepts for themselves, some inaccuracies or misconceptions may develop. When a teacher's assessment finds that a student is confused, which of the following is LEAST appropriate?

(A) The teacher can ask the student to review the evidence.

(B) The teacher can suggest that the student repeat the investigation, comparing new results with previous results.

(C) The teacher can tell the student to compare results in a small group of other students.

(D) The teacher can provide the correct answer(s) and praise the student for trying.

About the Question

In addition to the options listed above, in what other ways might a teacher help a student who is confused about a scientific concept? _____

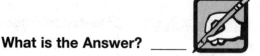

Explanation of the Answer

Students are often confused by new concepts. They may not understand new ideas the first time they are exposed to them. When they investigate new concepts for themselves and construct their own explanations for what they have "discovered," they may not reach valid conclusions. Teachers have to be able to identify common points of confusion or misconception among their students and then develop new ways to re-teach the material, while keeping students involved in their own learning and motivated to discover.

This question presents possible responses a teacher might make to students who are confused and asks you to select the LEAST appropriate response. In other words, which of the options will be the LEAST likely to motivate students in pursuing learning?

(A) is an appropriate teacher response. Children who are confused should be asked by the teacher to review the evidence (preferably by describing it to the teacher orally).

(B) is an appropriate teacher response. Teachers should encourage students to repeat their investigations when results are confusing—and to compare their new findings with their previous results.

(C) is an appropriate teacher response. Students should be encouraged to compare their results with the results of other students.

(D) is the correct answer. A teacher's goal should be to encourage students to actively discover answers for themselves and not to "get the right answer" from the teacher. Students are more likely to learn when they are actively involved. By providing "the answer," teachers are actually discouraging student involvement in their learning.

Beyond the Question

What techniques do you know for uncovering misconceptions in students' understanding? _____

_____

What techniques do you know for re-teaching to correct these misconceptions?

_____

_____

Why is it inappropriate for teachers to simply provide the correct answers for confused students? _____

_____

_____

PUTTING IT ALL TOGETHER

SCIENCE

Now that you have worked through this section of the workbook, you should have a general idea of what curriculum, instruction, and assessment issues are likely to appear on the test. The following chart is intended to help you think about the areas in which you might need further review before you take the test.

In addition, here is a list of topics that might appear on the test in the context of curriculum, instruction, and assessment in this subject area. Can you answer questions on these topics?

Sample Topics

- Observing similarities and differences in objects and events in the environment
- Describing objects and events in clear language
- Formulating hypotheses; planning, conducting, and explaining experiments; organizing data
- Model building and forecasting as they relate to science content
- Analysis of students' assumptions and misunderstandings in science
- Basic principles of health education
- Content-specific pedagogy

If you are working in a study group, you might try asking each other questions on these topics. You might also challenge each other to come up with questions based on the topics and on the specifications that appear throughout this section.

STUDY PLAN: SCIENCE

Content areas I need to study	Materials I have	Materials I need	Where can I find material I need?

4 SOCIAL STUDIES | *Curriculum, Instruction, Assessment*

Specification 1A | *Identify broad purposes for teaching all content areas and identify purposes for teaching particular topics within each content area. (For example, developing awareness of the world in social studies.)*

About the Specification

Look at your State Department of Education website for your state standards for social studies to see what the broad purposes for teaching social studies are in your state. (Chances are that your state's standards are similar to the National Social Studies standards as well.) According to your state's standards at the elementary level, what are the general purposes for students' learning in social studies?

_____

_____

_____

_____

sample question

One unit of the ten themes that form the National Social Studies Thematic Standards is "Time, Continuity, and Change." Which of the following questions for an upper elementary class would best address this theme?

(A) What are the locations of two major oil fields in the United States?

(B) In what kinds of places has oil been located?

(C) Why does drilling for oil cost so much?

(D) Why did the demand for oil increase with the mass production of the automobile?

About the Question

What is the goal behind the theme "Time, Continuity, and Change"?

_____

Why is the theme important in teaching social studies?

_____

What is the Answer? _____

Explanation of the Answer

Teachers must be familiar with the national standards in all of the fields in which they offer instruction, in addition to knowing the requirements of their school or district curricula. The national standards offer guidelines for teachers who are formulating instructional goals for their classes.

This question is designed to assess how well teacher candidates are able to translate national curricular standards into classroom instruction.

(A) While identifying locations might be part of a social studies lesson, it does not implement the theme of "Time, Continuity, and Change."

(B) Similarly, although naming places might be appropriate in a lesson, it does not implement the theme.

(C) Although this could be a useful question for students to consider, it does not implement the theme.

(D) is the correct answer. Asking why demand for oil increased with the invention of the automobile is a question that does implement the theme of "Time, Continuity, and Change." It asks students to analyze a historical event that has had profound consequences since it occurred, over a century ago. This is clearly the only one of the four options that offers this opportunity for analysis.

Beyond the Question

What kinds of topics might you pursue under the general category of "Time, Continuity, and Change" in a second-grade social studies class?

_____

_____

Specification 1B | Understand the relationship of subject area "parts" to subject area "wholes" for instructional planning and the instructional implications of these relationships.

About the Specification

Choose a grade level that you think you might like to teach. Look at a commonly-used social studies textbook at that level. (If you are currently enrolled in college, your adviser may tell you that you should look at a book that is now in use in school districts or you may be advised to look at new social studies books that reflect the latest thinking in teaching the subject.) Look at how the book divides the text into units and then look at the topics within the units. According to the textbook, what are some content area "wholes" (units)? What might their "parts" (topics) be?

Example 1:   The Colonial Period

    A. Customs of the Native Americans

    B. Customs of the immigrants—British, German, Dutch, French, and Spanish

    C. Tensions between Native Americans and immigrants

    D. Tensions between those loyal to England and those in favor of independence

Example 2:   Cultures of the World—the Aztecs

    A. Who the Aztecs were

    B. Where the Aztecs lived

    C. Customs and traditions of the Aztecs

    D. What happened to the Aztecs

Textbook Unit Topics: The Colonial Period

    A. _____

    B. _____

    C. _____

    D. _____

Textbook Unit Topics: Cultures of the World—the Aztecs

    A. _____

    B. _____

    C. _____

    D. _____

If you have an older social studies textbook and a new one, in what ways do their treatments of the curriculum differ?

_____

_____

A social studies teacher is planning a unit on the United States Constitution. Which of the following is she most likely to teach first?

(A) the Legislative Branch

(B) the Articles of Confederation

(C) the Bill of Rights

(D) the Executive Branch

About the Question

How does this question exemplify the specification? _____

_____

What is the subject area "whole" in this case? _____

_____

How are the "parts" related to the "whole"? _____

_____

How do the relationships help influence the sequencing of the parts? _____

_____

What is the Answer? _____

Explanation of the Answer

In social studies, as in all subject areas, it is important for teachers to understand how specific topics and units of study relate to their overall objectives and goals. The correct sequencing of topics is essential in order for concepts and skills to build upon each other and for a deeper understanding of themes. In this situation, you are to choose the topic MOST likely to be taught FIRST in a unit on the United States Constitution.

(B) is the correct answer. The Articles of Confederation were the first constitution adopted by the thirteen colonies and went into effect in 1781. Because the individual colonies (and then states) retained so much power, the articles left the national government fairly weak. Because of this situation, many problems arose, including "Shays' Rebellion," and the new Constitution was adopted with these defects in mind. Therefore, the Articles of Confederation are the best place to begin a unit on the United States Constitution. The other choices are all specific portions of the Constitution.

Beyond the Question

Choose a broad topic "whole" that you will be expected to teach in elementary social studies and then break it down into its component "parts."

Topic "whole" _____

Topic "parts" _____

_____

_____

Specification 1C	*Understand relationships among concepts both within and across content areas and the instructional implications of these interrelationships. (For example, the effects of geographical features on human cultures.)*

About the Specification

Think about how you might integrate the other content areas you are required to teach in elementary school into instruction in social studies (which is a particularly rich field for applying skills and knowledge from other areas).

How might you integrate language arts and social studies? _____

_____

How might you integrate science and social studies? _____

_____

How might you integrate music and social studies? _____

_____

How might you integrate physical education and social studies? _____

_____

_____

An upper elementary student selects a pie chart (or circle graph) to show the progression of changes in a town's population over a long period of time. Of the following, which statement is the most accurate assessment of the student's choice of a pie chart for this task?

(A) The student's choice is appropriate since a pie chart allows the student to display the data compactly.

(B) The student's choice is appropriate since a pie chart can be divided into as many time periods as needed.

(C) The student's choice is inappropriate since a pie chart is best used for contrasting and comparing.

(D) The student's choice is inappropriate since a pie chart requires the use of advanced mathematics.

About the Question

What kind of graphic representation would have best suited the student's data and purposes? _____

_____

Name one kind of information from a social studies unit that <u>could</u> be best represented in a pie chart. _____

_____

What is the Answer? _____

Explanation of the Answer

Teachers should be able to help students choose the best ways of representing data. Social studies students should be able to understand information and data that are represented visually—and they should be able to synthesize and present information and data themselves. In this question a student selects a pie chart as a way to represent the changes in a town's population over a long period of time. You are asked to evaluate the student's choice of the pie chart.

(C) is the correct answer. The pie chart is an inappropriate choice for the task of showing changes over a period of time. Line graphs and bar graphs should be selected when students want to show changes over time. Pie charts or circle graphs are good at showing relationships between the parts and the whole, and are therefore good for contrasting and comparing. A pie chart is not useful for showing changes over time. For that reason, it is not a good choice for the student.

Beyond the Question

It is important for teachers of social studies to help students become comfortable with interpreting (and creating) visual displays such as maps, charts, graphs, and tables. Where might you find materials that would help students build skills in this area? _____

_____

Specification	Identify types and uses of curricular materials, media and technologies, and other resources. (For example, maps and globes in social studies and such technology as video tapes and disks, computer software, and the Internet.)
1D	

About the Specification

Social studies allows for enrichment from outside sources. Think of a grade level you would like to teach, and then think of some specific resources that would enhance your teaching of social studies.

Grade level: _____

Videotapes: _____

Computer software: _____

Internet resources: _____

If you don't know about technological resources that you might use in teaching social studies, how might you find out about them? _____

_____

sample question

A third-grade teacher developed an activity that requires students to use a mileage chart to plan a trip through Germany. Students were supposed to arrange their routes to include all of the cities listed on the mileage chart with the least possible amount of driving. According to the K-5 scope and sequence of graphic skills pictured on the next page, is the teacher's goal likely or unlikely to be achieved?

(A) Likely, because the students have been previously taught all of the graphic skills needed by the time they reach third grade.

(B) Likely, because the students are always receptive to additional fun activities which involve materials other than the text.

(C) Unlikely, because the students would not be familiar with the country of Germany until the fifth grade.

(D) Unlikely, because the students would not be able to use the mileage chart to do the activity because it utilizes a skill that is not introduced until fourth grade.

Graphic Skills

#	Skill	K	1	2	3	4	5
	Grades						
1	Identifying and Comparing Features in Pictures/Photographs		♦	♦	♦	♦	♦
2	Interpreting Political Cartoons						♦
3	Identifying, Interpreting, and Comparing Lists		♦	♦	♦	♦	♦
4	Interpreting, Completing , and Comparing Tables				♦	♦	♦
5	Interpreting and Comparing Diagrams			♦	♦	♦	♦
6	Interpreting, Comparing, and Making Charts		♦	♦	♦	♦	♦
7	Using and Making Flowcharts			♦	♦	♦	♦
8	Reading a Mileage Chart					♦	♦
9	Reading Schedules and Calendars		♦	♦	♦	♦	♦
10	Interpreting and Making Pictographs		♦	♦	♦	♦	♦
11	Interpreting, Comparing, and Making Bar Graphs			♦	♦	♦	♦
12	Interpreting, Comparing, and Making Line Graphs					♦	♦
13	Interpreting, Comparing, and Making Circle Graphs					♦	♦
14	Identifying and Reading Climographs						
15	Comparing Graphs and Tables				♦	♦	♦

About the Question

One of the teacher's goals is probably to introduce students to cities in Germany. What other activities could the teacher use to reach this goal?

_____

_____

What is the Answer? _____

Explanation of the Answer

Teachers must always bear in mind whether their students are educationally and developmentally ready for the lessons they are planning. "Can my students understand this lesson?" is a question that teachers must constantly ask.

In the scenario presented in this question, you are asked to evaluate whether an activity planned by a third-grade teacher is "likely" or "unlikely" to be achieved, and why. Here you must consult the scope and sequence of graphic skills presented on the accompanying chart and analyze which skills are required by the teacher's assignment. After you have done that, you must select the appropriate answer.

(A) From studying the chart you can see that it is not true that third-grade students "have been previously taught all of the graphic skills needed." Because they have not been taught to read a mileage chart, they are unlikely to have success with the assignment.

(B) Whether or not this is a "fun" activity for students, the fact is that they have not been taught how to read a mileage chart.

(C) The chart does not indicate whether students would "be familiar with the country of Germany until the fifth grade," but the fact remains that they have not been taught how to read a mileage chart.

(D) is the correct answer. The key point is that, according to the table, reading a mileage chart is a graphic skill that is not taught until fourth grade. Therefore, third-grade students are not likely to have this skill. The teacher's planned activity is NOT appropriate for the grade level and the teacher's goal is, therefore, NOT likely to be achieved.

Beyond the Question

Based on your knowledge of third graders' skills, is there another way to incorporate trip planning into a social studies lesson <u>without</u> using a mileage chart? Where else could students pretend to travel? What resources would you need for such an activity? _____

_____

_____

_____

INSTRUCTION

Specification	Demonstrate knowledge of methods of identifying, assessing, activating, and building on the students' prior knowledge, experiences, cultural backgrounds, and skills in each content area.
2A	

About the specification

Cultural differences are a particularly relevant topic for social studies. At the very beginning of the school year, what are some ways that you can become familiar with (and sensitive to) your students' cultural backgrounds?

_____

_____

_____

A fourth-grade teacher is planning a unit on the history of the state in which the students live. Prior to beginning the unit, the teacher wants to assess the students' overall general knowledge of state history. Which of the following activities would be most likely to meet this goal?

(A) Have students brainstorm as a group what they know about the state's history

(B) Have each student make a list of important events in the state's history

(C) Have each student choose an event in the state's history and write an essay about why it was important

(D) Have students interview older people in the community about what life was like long ago in the state

About the Question

What is "brainstorming"? _____

When is brainstorming <u>most</u> useful? _____

When is brainstorming <u>least</u> useful? _____

What is the Answer? _____

Explanation of the Answer

"Assessment" is a continuum, from formal to informal. Here a fourth-grade teacher wants to assess a class's prior knowledge of state history before beginning a new unit of study. This is a common situation in the classroom. It calls for an assessment technique that is not complicated or time-consuming.

(A) is the correct answer. Although all of the techniques listed could be used as assessment techniques, only brainstorming meets the needs of the teacher for a simple but effective method of finding out what the students already know.

Beyond the Question

When might you want to assign answer choice B to a class?_____

_____

When might you want to assign answer choice D to the class? _____

_____

_____

Specification

2B | Demonstrate knowledge of methods of preparing, evaluating, and justifying instructional activities within and across content areas

About the Specification

Teachers need to know why they are doing what they are doing in class—not just something that is fun for students, but activities that meet curriculum goals and are instructionally appropriate for learning.

Think of a social studies unit you might teach at a specific grade level.

*Grade level*_____ *Unit to teach* _____

How would you structure activities throughout the unit to meet the goals of the unit?

Instructional goals _____

Activity 1: _____

Activity 2: _____

Activity 3: _____

Activity 4: _____

Activity 5: _____

This is exactly what effective teachers do for every subject and every unit. Sound knowledge of structuring activities to meet a known goal will help your students learn to the best of their abilities.

sample question

As part of a social studies unit on Aztec culture, a lower elementary teacher has students make papier mache masks that resemble those used by the Aztec peoples in ritual dances. This is an example of which of the following?

(A) Content integration

(B) Assessing prior knowledge

(C) Brainstorming

(D) Using metacognitive skills

About the Question

How does the making of masks and learning about ritual dances fit into learning about the Aztec culture? _____

_____

_____

What is the Answer? ____

Explanation of the Answer

Test takers must be prepared to answer questions that deal with instructional activities, and with methods of preparing, evaluating, and justifying those activities. Here you are presented with a scenario and asked to identify the type of instructional activity that is being utilized by the teacher.

(A) is the correct answer. "Content integration" is the appropriate term for the activity presented in this scenario, where students use art to explore another culture as part of a social sciences unit.

(B) "Assessing prior knowledge" is a term applied to evaluating what students already know.

(C) "Brainstorming" is a term that describes the activity of a group of students who have been asked to respond to a question orally, in which the teacher usually writes the responses on a chalkboard without making judgments about them.

(D) "Using metacognitive skills" refers to "thinking about thinking"—asking students to analyze their thought processes.

Beyond the Question

What would the teacher need to do during and after the masks were being made to be sure that students were actually learning about Aztec culture?

_____

_____

_____

Specification
2C Select teaching and learning strategies to help individual students or groups of students understand topics and concepts within content areas. (For example, demonstration; cooperative learning; guided oral and silent work; use of journals and logs; graphic organizers; and inquiry method.)

About the Specification

This specification is concerned with meeting the needs of <u>all</u> students and giving all learners an equal opportunity in class. It recognizes that there are different ways of helping students learn and that there are different methods for meeting students' varying needs.

When might you use demonstration in teaching social studies?_____

_____

When might you use guided oral and silent work?_____

_____

How might journals be useful for students' learning in social studies? _____

_____

sample question

Which of the following is likely to be most beneficial for students having difficulty understanding the concept of checks and balances ?

(A) Have the students compare the responsibilities of the different branches of the national government with those of their state's government.

(B) Have a group of students make rules for the class, have another group interpret the rules, and have one student make sure that the rules are carried out.

(C) Have students read their state's constitution and write an essay about some of the state's major problems.

(D) Have students read the section of their textbook dealing with checks and balances, taking notes and looking up all unfamiliar vocabulary words.

About the Question

What is "the concept of checks and balances"?_____

_____

What social studies area or unit includes the study of this concept?_____

_____

What is the Answer? ____

Explanation of the Answer

This is a question about teaching strategies. It asks about what is "likely to be most beneficial for students" in understanding the concept of checks and balances. Although each of the possible activities might have merit as an activity, one is clearly the most effective way to teach this concept.

(B) is the correct answer. This is the most effective way to teach the concept. It is the one that most actively involves students and it is the most personal, based on the actual experiences of students. It is the most likely to result in true understanding of the concept.

Beyond the Question

What other concepts might you be likely to teach at the same time that you teach about checks and balances? _____

_____

Specification	
2D	*Demonstrate knowledge of methods of adjusting instruction to meet students' needs. (For example, corrective and developmental instruction; re-teaching; follow-up and enrichment instruction; and preparation of content area instruction to meet the needs of all readers.)*

About the Specification

The reality of many elementary classrooms today is that they contain students of varying abilities and different backgrounds. That's why knowledge of how to adjust instruction is so important.

Think of a unit that you might teach in social studies (for example, life in the Colonial, or pre-Revolutionary, period). Think of a grade level you might teach. Then think about ways of meeting the needs of all learners in teaching that unit.

Social studies unit: _____ Grade level: _____

How would you teach developmental learners (those who are below grade level in reading skill, for example)? _____

_____

How would you teach learners who are at grade level? _____

_____

How would you teach learners with more background knowledge of this subject than the rest of the class? _____

_____

How would you teach learners whose primary language is not English and whose skills in English are limited?_____

At the end of a unit on nineteenth-century and early twentieth-century immigration to the United States, several children express a desire to explore the ideas of the unit further. Of the following, which is most likely to provide these students with enrichment activities that require their use of critical thinking skills on this topic?

(A) Asking the students to draw posters about cities that were greatly affected by immigration

(B) Providing the students with photos of newly-arrived immigrants at Ellis Island and asking them to write stories that describe these immigrants' lives

(C) Having the students find words in the dictionary that come from other languages

(D) Assigning the students a variety of historical fiction from the nineteenth-century for them to read independently

About the Question

What are "critical thinking skills"?_____

In general, how can you structure assignments to enhance critical thinking skills?

_____

_____

What is the Answer? _____

Explanation of the Answer

Teachers are constantly required to adjust their methods of instruction to meet the specific needs of their students. All successful teachers are able to create meaningful work for their students that is likely to result in true learning. Here, for example, the teacher wants to encourage a group of students to pursue their interests in U.S. immigration history. You are asked to select the activity that is most likely to result in critical thinking (and, therefore, learning).

(B) is the correct answer. Although each of the other possible activities might have merit as an assignment, only this activity engages students in critical thinking. They have to truly engage with the life situations of immigrants to be able to write about them.

Beyond the Question

What social studies unit would you expect to follow the unit on immigration that is described above? _____

_____

Why? _____

Specification

2E

Demonstrate knowledge of various strategies for motivating students and encouraging their success. (For example, praise, wait time, token economies, and student choice.)

About the Specification

What are some reasons that elementary students might not engage with social studies? _____

_____

What are some strategies that you think are effective in engaging students in learning about social studies topics? _____

_____

sample question

A fifth-grade teacher has been reviewing the main events that led up to the American Revolutionary War from 1750. The teacher has assigned students a timeline to create individually. Which of the following strategies is the most educationally appropriate for motivating all of the students in the class to create accurate timelines?

(A) Place a colorful sticker on the timelines that are accurate.

(B) Allow the class to act out a short, fun historical play if ninety percent of the students turn in accurate timelines.

(C) Tell the students who turn in accurate timelines what a great job they did.

(D) Give the students who turn in accurate timelines an extra five minutes of recess.

About the Question

What is the teacher trying to motivate?_____

_____

"Motivation" is not always about motivating students to <u>like</u> something. It's also about motivating them to engage with the task and to do their best work.

Explanation of the Answer

Teachers have many strategies for motivating students, and teachers should know how to utilize age-appropriate strategies to encourage the success of their students. In this question, fifth-grade students are to complete timelines. Your task is to identify the "MOST educationally appropriate" strategy the teacher can employ to motivate the students.

(B) is the correct answer. This is the most educationally appropriate strategy. It rewards students with an activity that is both fun and educational, and it is the most likely to motivate the entire class.

Beyond the Question

Many candidates (and practicing teachers as well) are tempted to say that an extra five minutes of recess is far more motivating than any of the other choices. Why isn't (D) the correct answer? _____

What is a possible negative consequence of continually motivating students with extra recess or with rewards of candy? _____

_____

Specification
2F

Demonstrates knowledge of a variety of approaches to instruction and the theoretical and empirical bases of these approaches. (For example, developmentally appropriate instruction and model-based classroom management.)

About the Specification

What are some approaches to social studies instruction that have been shown to be effective in the early elementary grades? _____

_____

_____

Give specific examples of classroom instruction based on the approaches you listed above. _____

_____

_____

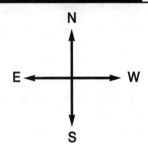

N

E ← → W

S

After a geography lesson on cardinal points, nearly one-half of the students in a first-grade class label a compass as shown above. Which of the following is the LEAST developmentally appropriate strategy to help these students?

(A) Place an "E" sticker on the students' right hands and a "W" sticker on their left hands.

(B) Have students use hand-held compasses to find their way around the school.

(C) Teach students a song that names each direction as they move clockwise around a compass on the floor.

(D) Assign students to locate and list ten cities in the eastern hemisphere and ten in the western.

TIP: It is important for candidates to be aware of the age of the students in a question. Many answers that initially appear correct are obviously wrong when age is taken into consideration.

About the Question

It can be difficult to teach geography to first graders. Can you think of additional activities that explain cardinal points in an age-appropriate manner?

What is the Answer? _____

Explanation of the Answer

Teachers must not only utilize a variety of instructional techniques in the classroom, but they must also be sure that the techniques are developmentally appropriate for the particular students. In this question, almost fifty percent of first-grade students are incorrectly labeling a compass. You are to determine the "LEAST developmentally appropriate strategy" the teacher can use to help these first-graders.

(D) is the correct answer. This is not a developmentally appropriate strategy for first-graders. The assignment is too abstract for students of this age, who would not have a good concept of hemispheres. All the other activities are more appropriate for these students, since each one has a concrete task to encourage learning.

Beyond the Question

What happens developmentally to upper elementary students that allows instruction to be different from that used with lower elementary students?

_____

_____

In what ways can instruction be different for upper elementary students, even if the topics are similar?

_____

_____

_____

ASSESSMENT

Specification

3A _Demonstrate knowledge of when and how to use traditional and standardized testing methodologies. (For example, standardized tests, publisher-produced tests, screening tests.)_

About the Specification

What standardized tests in social studies do elementary students in your state usually take?

_____

How can you make standardized testing a useful exercise for your students (and for their parents)?

_____

_____

_____

A third-grade class is learning about the 50 states of the United States and their capitals. The teacher uses a variety of independent, whole class, and at-home learning activities to meet the objectives of the unit. After testing the students on all of the objectives, individual student performance is compared to the performance of the other students in the class.

The evaluation described above is best characterized as which of the following?

    I.   Formative

    II. Summative

    III. Norm-referenced

    IV. Criterion-referenced

(A) I and III

(B) I and IV

(C) II and III

(D) II and IV

About the Question

What is a possible purpose of comparing individual student performance to the performance of other students in the class?

_____

Comparing the performance of students in the class is related to "grading on a curve." What assumptions is a teacher making when he or she plans to "grade on a curve"?

_____

What is the Answer? _____

Explanation of the Answer

There are many methods of assessing student learning. Teachers are expected to understand and apply appropriate testing methodologies. In this example, a teacher uses a variety of learning activities and methods of assessing individual performance. The teacher then compares individual performance to the performance of the class as a whole.

(C) is the correct answer. First, the teacher uses a "summative" assessment, assessing the "sum" of the objectives to see how well students have mastered them, and using this information to grade the students on their learning. By then comparing individual vs. class performance statistics, the teacher is using "norm-referenced" assessment.

"Formative" assessment is giving students feedback designed to help them increase their skills, without the consequences of grading.

"Criterion-referenced" assessment is based on a standard (a "criterion") and is not based on a relationship to the performance of others.

Beyond the Question

What does "standardized test" mean? What qualifies a test as "standardized"? _____

_____

When is a test NOT a standardized test? _____

_____

What would have made the end-of-unit test in the question above a criterion-referenced test rather than a norm-referenced test? _____

_____

Specification 3B	Demonstrate knowledge of various classroom-based, informal, or nontraditional assessment strategies. (For example, observation; oral reports; running records; informal reading inventories; portfolios; and performance samples.)

About the Specification

What kinds of behaviors could you observe in social studies classes?

_____

What might you assess when observing these behaviors?

_____

What kind of "performance sample" might you require in social studies?

_____

What would you look for and assess in these performance samples?

_____

What kind(s) of portfolios might be useful in social studies classes?

_____

_____

_____

An upper elementary grade student was asked to use a map of the western hemisphere to answer questions about places, landmarks, and geographical features. This activity would best assess which of the following social studies skills?

(A) Building models and hypotheses

(B) Interpreting graphic representations

(C) Understanding the lessons of history

(D) Predicting data outcomes

About the Question

Why is reading and understanding maps an important part of social studies?

What is the Answer? _____

Explanation of the Answer

Social studies students are expected to be able to answer questions about "places, landmarks, and geographical features." Using a map to assess their understanding is entirely appropriate.

(B) is the correct answer. A map is a form of "graphic representation." Social studies students are expected to be able to understand graphic representations of information, including data presented in maps, charts, and graphs.

Beyond the Question

Look again at the specification above. What kind of assessment is described in this question? _____

_____

What other kinds of assessments in social studies might involve reading and interpreting maps? _____

_____

Specification | *Interpret data obtained from various formal and informal assessments.*

3C

About the specification

What are "data"? _____

_____

What "data" would the teacher receive from the assessment described in the question above (3B)?_____

_____

What are some challenges to the teacher in interpreting data like that collected in the question above (3B)? _____

_____

sample question

A fourth-grade teacher gave an end-of-unit test on the various methods of transportation before the twentieth century. The test consisted of several multiple-choice questions and two essays to be written from a range of topics. Most of the students did very well on the multiple-choice questions but poorly on the essays. Which of the following teacher responses would be the most appropriate?

(A) Review general essay writing, have students write and assess a few sample essays, then re-administer a new essay test on transportation.

(B) Move on to methods of transportation in the twentieth century, but do not include essays as part of the assessment.

(C) Review all the material and give another complete test, with multiple-choice and essay questions.

(D) Give grades based only on the multiple-choice section.

About the Question

Why might students do well on multiple-choice questions but poorly on essays? _____

_____

What is the Answer? _____

Explanation of the Answer

There are many ways for a teacher to assess students. It is just as important for the teacher to know how to interpret the results as it is to know which type of assessment to use. In this scenario, a teacher gets mixed results from an assessment on methods of transportation. You are to determine which teacher response is the MOST appropriate.

(A) is the correct answer. Essay writing is frequently difficult for elementary-age students. Even though they may know the material well enough to answer multiple choice or fill-in-the-blank questions, they will often do poorly on essay questions. Essays require clarity of thought, adequate preparation, and direct writing that goes well beyond a surface understanding of the topic—and they require practice. A review, practice, and reassessment would be the most appropriate response.

(B) Effective teachers should not be tempted to leave out difficult areas of instruction. Quality essay writing is a key part of an overall education.

(C) The problem is not with all the material but with the essay response. Remember, the students had a range of topics from which to choose and the majority still did poorly on their essays. It is the essay portion of the test that needs to be readministered.

(D) Effective teachers will not ignore the areas where their students are having difficulties. The primary purpose of tests is not to give grades, but to assess what students have learned and to discover where they are having difficulties in understanding.

Beyond the Question

What are some factors that prevent teachers from choosing the best follow-up action after their assessments? _____

_____

What advice would you give to a teacher who does not choose the best follow-up action after an assessment? _____

_____

Specification	Identify common points of confusion or misconception among
3D	elementary school learners in the various content areas. (For example, errors and patterns of error; inaccurate factual knowledge or vocabulary; misconceptions about processes or relationships; "buggy" algorithms.)

About the Specification

What are some common problems or misconceptions that elementary school students are likely to have in social studies?

_____

_____

How can you assess students to uncover common problems?

_____

_____

_____

When students were asked to name three human needs, the teacher received the following responses:

STUDENT A	STUDENT B	STUDENT C	STUDENT D
basketball	doll house	car	food
pizza	parents	video game	clothes
camcorder	dresses	house	air

Which list demonstrates an understanding of human needs versus human wants?

(A) basketball, pizza, camcorder

(B) doll house, parents, dresses

(C) car, video game, house

(D) food, clothes, air

About the Question

Are these students more likely to be lower-elementary or upper-elementary students? How do you know?_____
_____

What is the Answer? _____

Explanation of the Answer

There are many ways for a teacher to assess common points of confusion or misconception among elementary school students. In this question, the teacher wanted to know whether students understood the difference between human "needs" and human "wants." Four of the lists produced by students are reproduced in the question.

(D) is the correct answer. This is the only list that demonstrates an understanding of human "needs." All of the others are lists of "wants."

Beyond the Question

What are some ways of making sure that students understand important terms and concepts in social studies?

_____
_____
_____

PUTTING IT ALL TOGETHER

SOCIAL STUDIES

Now that you have worked through this section of the workbook, you should have a general idea of what curriculum, instruction, and assessment issues are likely to appear on the test. The following chart is intended to help you think about the areas in which you might need further review before you take the test.

In addition, here is a list of topics that might appear on the test in the context of curriculum, instruction, and assessment in this subject area. Can you answer questions on these topics?

Sample Topics

- Human behavior in society
- Social organizations
- Government
- Social structures, including communication, transportation, industrialization, technology, and economics
- Skills: organizing data, problem solving, comparing and contrasting, model building, planning, and forecasting (as they relate to social studies content)
- Students' development of appropriate concepts in social studies
- Content-specific pedagogy

If you are working in a study group, you might try asking each other questions on these topics. You might also challenge each other to come up with questions based on the topics and on the specifications that appear throughout this section.

STUDY PLAN: SOCIAL STUDIES

Content areas I need to study	Materials I have	Materials I need	Where can I find material I need?

STUDY PLAN: SOCIAL STUDIES

Content areas I need to study	Materials I have	Materials I need	Where can I find material I need?

ARTS AND PHYSICAL EDUCATION

Curriculum, Instruction, Assessment

5

Specification 1A

Identify broad purposes for teaching all content areas and identify purposes for teaching particular topics within each content area.

About the Specification

This section covers music, art, and physical education. Check to see whether your state has standards for these three content areas and become familiar with those standards.

What are some general purposes for teaching music in elementary school?

_____

_____

_____

What are some general purposes for teaching art in elementary school?

_____

_____

_____

What are some general purposes for teaching physical education in elementary school?

_____

_____

_____

As elementary school students progress in the area of art production, it is LEAST important for them to develop the ability to

(A) use art materials effectively

(B) employ multiple processes in artwork

(C) see relationships among their work, their world, and their imaginations

(D) represent figures and objects with a high degree of accuracy

About the Question

Look at the general purposes for teaching art that you noted above. Do they relate to the possible answers to this question? What are some activities that might help students achieve the goals you have for them?

General Goal   *Possible Activity*

_____   _____

_____   _____

_____   _____

_____   _____

What is the Answer? _____

Explanation of the Answer

Elementary education teachers are facilitators of student learning. They have to know what learning goals are appropriate for their students. This question inquires about appropriate goals for teachers who are facilitating student progress in art. It asks which of the goals is LEAST important. The phrasing of the question tells you that three out of the four possible goals are appropriate, while only one is not. It is this one that is the answer to the question.

(D) is the correct answer. It is generally thought that elementary students do NOT have to be able to represent figures and objects with a high degree of accuracy. All of the other possible answers describe skills that are more important than accurate representation.

Beyond the Question

Choose a grade you would like to teach: _____

What do you know about the music curriculum for this grade?_____

_____

What would you be required to teach in art at this grade level? _____

_____

What would you be required to teach in physical education? _____

_____

If you don't know what you would be required to teach in any of these subjects, how might you find out? _____

_____

| Specification 1B | *Understand the relationship of subject area "parts" to subject area "wholes" for instructional planning and the instructional implications of these relationships.* |

About the Specification

Choose ONE of the three content areas that interests you—music, art, or physical education. Talk with your faculty adviser or with a practicing teacher at a grade level that interests you. For the subject at that grade level, find out what the "wholes" and "parts" are. What are the broad goals of the curriculum and what are the specific topics you will be expected to teach?

For example: in fifth-grade music you might be asked to teach students to recognize the instruments that make up an orchestra. The parts of that "whole" might involve finding ways for students to hear and see different instruments.

Content area _____   Grade level _____

Content area "whole" (curriculum goal)   Content area "parts" (topics)

_____   _____

_____   _____

_____   _____

_____   _____

_____   _____

A physical education teacher is planning a unit on basketball. Which of the following is this teacher most likely to teach last?

(A) some simple offensive plays

(B) dribbling the ball

(C) passing the ball

(D) how to shoot a lay-up

About the Question

What does this question assume about the content area "part" to be taught last? _____

_____

If you don't know basketball well, you should still be able to answer this question. What reasoning can you use to find the correct answer? _____

_____

What is the Answer? _____

Explanation of the Answer

When planning units of instruction, it is important for the teacher to be aware of the sequence as well as the content of the material. At times, lessons build on previous information or skills. At other times, lessons are developmentally appropriate for students only at a specific age. This question asks you to identify the sequencing of a basketball unit planned by a physical education teacher.

(A) is the correct answer. The teacher will most probably give instruction on team plays last, after basic individual skills have been developed. All the other answers are individual skills and need to be developed before team play.

Beyond the Question

Assuming that you might be asked to teach soccer, softball (or tee-ball), kickball, and volleyball in elementary school, what skills would you probably be required to teach for each sport?

Soccer	*Softball*	*Kickball*	*Volleyball*
_____	_____	_____	_____
_____	_____	_____	_____
_____	_____	_____	_____
_____	_____	_____	_____

Now put numbers (1 - 4) next to the skills listed in each column, indicating the order in which the skills should be taught (number 1 first, number 2 second, etc.)

| Specification | Understand relationships among concepts both within and |
| 1C | across content areas and the instructional implications of these interrelationships. |

About the Specification

What relationships can you think of between music and language arts? (Be specific.)

_____

What about relationships between social studies and physical education?

_____

Between art and science? _____

Between art and math? _____

sample question

Which of the following is the best example of an interdisciplinary activity in mathematics and physical education for fourth-grade students?

(A) conducting a mathematics class outside on a warm spring day

(B) encouraging all students to keep score during a baseball game

(C) calculating the ideal trajectory for a basketball free throw

(D) keeping a record of students' long-jump distances and graphing the results

About the Question

What is an "interdisciplinary activity"? _____

_____

Can you think of other interdisciplinary activities that integrate mathematics and physical education? _____

_____

What is the Answer? _____

Explanation of the Answer

Effective elementary school teachers help students connect their learning from one subject area to another. They assist students in applying what they have learned. This question presents a fine example: here the teacher is integrating mathematics skills into a physical education activity.

(A) doesn't actually integrate mathematics and physical education. Here the teacher is simply moving the mathematics class outdoors.

(B) although there is some basic arithmetic involved in keeping score in a baseball game, this isn't really displaying an integration of mathematics knowledge with a physical education lesson.

(C) calculating the ideal trajectory for a free throw involves mathematical calculations that are beyond the ability of most fourth graders.

(D) is the correct answer. Fourth graders can certainly keep track of the distances they jump and can then apply their mathematics skills in creating a graph that shows the overall results of their jumps.

Beyond the Question

Why is it important to integrate music, art, and physical education with language arts, mathematics, social studies, and science?

_____

_____

Specification	Identify types and uses of curricular materials, media and technologies, and other resources.
1D	

About the Specification

What kinds of curricular materials and technologies can a teacher use for teaching art, in addition to materials like clay, paint, crayons, etc.?

_____

What kinds of media and technologies can a teacher use for teaching music, in addition to showing and playing instruments?

_____

What kinds of materials, media, and technologies can a teacher use for teaching physical education, in addition to balls, bats, goals, etc.?

_____

sample question

Which of the following is LEAST likely to be included in a unit on stringed instruments?

(A) an audio tape of Spanish guitar music

(B) a videotape of people playing violins

(C) a teacher playing the piano

(D) a teacher playing the banjo

About the Question

To successfully teach music in elementary school, you will need to know "families" of musical instruments. Take a minute to list below some of the "families" you know, and list some examples of instruments in each family.

"Family" of Instruments   *Examples of Instruments*

_____   _____

                                          _____

                                          _____

_____   _____

                                          _____

                                          _____

What is the Answer? _____

Explanation of the Answer

Teachers should be aware of materials and resources available to them and of their proper use. In this example, you are asked to identify which resource a music teacher is LEAST likely to employ while teaching a unit on stringed instruments.

(C) is the correct answer. A piano is a percussion instrument—felt-covered hammers hit strings to make sounds. All the other choices do involve stringed instruments and are appropriate to use in this unit.

TIP: It is important for the elementary teacher to have an understanding of the basic concepts and materials used by special area teachers, including Art, Music, and Physical Education. If you have not "brushed up" on fundamental concepts in these areas, you should do so before you take the test.

Beyond the Question

How might you teach a lesson on stringed instruments if you cannot play one yourself? _____

_____

INSTRUCTION

Specification

2A

Demonstrate knowledge of methods of identifying, assessing, activating, and building on the students' prior knowledge, experiences, cultural backgrounds, and skills in each content area.

About the Specification

How can you identify students' prior knowledge and experiences in music?

_____

How can you identify students' prior knowledge and experiences in art?

_____

How can you identify students' prior knowledge and experiences in physical education?

_____

How might cultural differences have an impact on instruction in these three areas?

In music: _____

In art: _____

In physical education: _____

sample question

Which of the following is the most appropriate statement to make to students who will be engaging in a brainstorming activity in their art class?

(A) "Say only your very best ideas."

(B) "We want original ideas from your own mind."

(C) "Don't judge ideas now; we can do that later."

(D) "Make sure your ideas make sense before saying them."

About the Question

What might students "brainstorm" about in an art class? What questions might the teacher ask? _____

_____

What is the Answer? _____

Explanation of the Answer

Brainstorming is an important instructional technique. It is a simple way of identifying and assessing what students know. At the same time, it is a useful "readiness" activity that can stimulate students and prepare them to learn. In this question, you are presented with four possible statements that a teacher might make to students before they begin brainstorming. You are asked to select the most appropriate statement.

(C) is the correct answer. Brainstorming is most useful for teachers when it is most spontaneous. Students should be encouraged to contribute their ideas on a topic or answers to a question without "pre-screening" their responses. This allows the teacher to see more accurately what the students know or believe. The statements labeled (A), (B), and (D) all ask students to screen what they say before they say it. Only statement (C) accurately reflects the goal of brainstorming: "Don't judge ideas now; we can do that later."

Beyond the Question

What questions in music and physical education might be used to initiate a brainstorming session?

In music: _____

In physical education:_____

| Specification | Demonstrate knowledge of methods of preparing, evaluating, and justifying instructional activities within and across content areas. |
| 2B | |

About the Specification

As a teacher, you will encounter practical problems that will challenge your instructional plans. What kinds of challenges can you envision in the three subject areas?

In music _____

In art: _____

In physical education: _____

For a music lesson on how sounds are created, a teacher has groups of students create simple musical instruments and demonstrate together how to play them. The form of instruction being used can best be described as

(A) experimenting

(B) cooperative learning

(C) portfolio assessment

(D) lecturing

About the Question

It is quite possible that this teacher is overcoming a practical problem in designing this activity. What are some of the challenges that the teacher might have encountered? _____

What is the Answer? _____

Explanation of the Answer

Instruction should take place in many ways. No single technique is the correct one for every subject. In fact, the effective teacher will have many methods of instructing students. In the scenario presented here, the teacher has groups of students create simple musical instruments and then demonstrate how to play them. You are asked to identify the technique that the teacher is using in this activity.

(B) is the correct answer. Using groups to create and demonstrate musical instruments is an example of cooperative learning; that is, learning activities in which students must work together to produce a result.

Beyond the Question

What might the teacher do next to reinforce the students' understanding of how sounds are created? _____

Specification

2C

Select teaching and learning strategies to help individual students or groups of students understand topics and concepts within content areas. (For example: demonstration; cooperative learning; guided oral and silent work; use of journals and logs; graphic organizers; and inquiry method.)

About the Specification

Which strategies used as examples in the specification above do you think would be the most effective for teaching music? Why? _____

_____

_____

Which strategies would be the most effective for teaching art? Why? _____

_____

_____

Which strategies would be the most effective for teaching physical education? Why?

_____

_____

sample question

A visual learner is having difficulty remembering the various major groups of orchestral instruments. Which of the following teaching and learning strategies would best help this student?

(A) cooperative learning

(B) think-pair-share

(C) a graphic organizer

(D) a lecture

About the Question

In general, what strategies can teachers employ in their lessons to meet the needs of visual learners? _____

_____

What is the Answer? _____

Explanation of the Answer

Knowing a broad range of teaching and learning strategies can benefit every teacher. Teachers must be able to select the methods of instruction that are likely to benefit all of their students. In this example, you are to decide which strategy would best help a "visual learner."

(A) Cooperative learning is a way in which students must work together to produce a result. It is not a relevant answer to this question.

(B) Think-pair-share involves individual students thinking about a topic or problem, pairing up with fellow students to compare ideas, and then sharing their thoughts and findings with a larger group or with the whole class. It is not a technique that is particularly helpful to a visual learner because it is primarily auditory.

(C) is the correct answer. Graphic organizers, webs, charts, etc. all help the visual learner because information is organized in a display that makes it easier for these students to see relationships and understand concepts.

(D) Lectures are not as helpful to the visual learner, since they rely on auditory and not visual processing.

Beyond the Question

Imagine that, just before school starts in the fall, the budget for art is eliminated at the school where you are to begin teaching—but the time for teaching art is left in the curriculum. Think of a grade level that you might be teaching. Now imagine how you might teach art without a budget. In other words, what art concepts might you teach without materials, and how might you teach these?

Grade Level _____

Art Concepts	*Instructional Techniques*
_____	_____
_____	_____
_____	_____

Specification 2D	*Demonstrate knowledge of methods of adjusting instruction to meet students' needs. (For example: corrective and developmental instruction; re-teaching; follow-up and enrichment instruction; and preparation of content area instruction to meet the needs of all readers.)*

About the Specification

Students in elementary school have widely varying levels of skill in music, art, and physical education. What might you do as a teacher of physical education with students who are not as physically coordinated as most of the other students in your class? _____

_____

_____

How might a teacher best help a child who always sings off-key?

(A) Encourage the child to sing as softly as possible

(B) Praise the student generously

(C) Utilize learning activities such as tone-matching games

(D) Assign music for the child to listen to at home

About the Question

Just as students differ in their athletic skills, they also differ in their musical skills. Can you think of other educationally-appropriate suggestions that this teacher might make to a child who always sings off-key?

What is the Answer? _____

Explanation of the Answer

Effective teachers will be able to identify students who are not learning the material that is being taught. For these students, teachers must be able to find different ways of presenting the material until the student has demonstrated mastery. Here you are asked how a teacher might best help a student who does not sing on key. You must select the strategy that is most likely to be successful.

(A) is not the correct answer. Encouraging the child to sing softly does not help him or her learn to sing on key.

(B) is not the correct answer. While being generous with praise is sometimes the most appropriate action for a teacher to take, it will not help this child learn to sing on key.

(C) is the correct answer. Utilizing games that involve matching tones is the most likely of the four options to assist the student in learning to sing on key.

(D) is not the correct answer. Asking the child to listen to assigned music at home is not likely to help him or her to learn to sing on key.

TIP: You must always find the ONE answer that best answers the specific question being asked. Although several of the actions described might be appropriate learning interventions in other situations, only ONE is most likely to be successful with this particular student in this specific scenario.

Beyond the Question

What would you do to accommodate a child with limited mobility in a music, art, or physical education class?

_____

_____

| Specification | Demonstrate knowledge of various strategies for motivating |
| 2E | students and encouraging their success. (For example: praise, wait time, token economies, and student choice.) |

About the Specification

Because music, art, and physical education often involve performance-based activities, motivating students who are overly critical of their own performances can be a challenge. On the other hand, some students see music, art, and physical education classes as "play time."

What are some ways of motivating (and supporting) students who are extremely self-critical in these content areas? _____

_____

_____

What are some ways of helping students understand that, while these content areas can be fun, they are not "time off" from school? _____

_____

_____

sample question

An elementary school music teacher finds that band students love playing upbeat, popular tunes and are not enthusiastic about playing classical music. The teacher hears protests whenever students are asked to play a classical piece. The teacher decides to tell students: "If you do a good job on this piece, one time through, then we will play one song of your choice."

This teacher is demonstrating which of the following?

(A) Wait time

(B) Positive reinforcement

(C) Token economies

(D) Time out

About the Question

This teacher faces a challenge that you are likely to face as a teacher. What other actions might the teacher have taken with the band? _____

_____

What is the Answer? _____

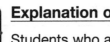

Explanation of the Answer

Students who are motivated are students who are ready to learn. Teachers must be familiar with a variety of strategies to motivate their students. Here a teacher is faced with students who are not motivated to play classical music, even though it is a required part of the curriculum. The challenge for the teacher is to find a way to motivate these students—and the teacher is successful. Your challenge is to identify the strategy that the teacher uses.

(A) is not the correct answer. "Wait time" generally refers to asking a question (sometimes by asking a specific student) and then pausing to allow some thinking time before asking the question again (or calling on another student).

(B) is the correct answer. The teacher's strategy is an example of "positive reinforcement." The teacher is offering the students the opportunity to do something they like to do (play popular music) if they will first do something they don't like as much (play classical music). In other words, the students will receive a reward from the teacher (and will therefore be "positively reinforced" in their behavior).

(C) is not the correct answer. "Token economies" generally refers to setting up a system that distributes "tokens" ("play money" or colored chips, for example) to students for their achievements or accomplishments.

(D) is not the correct answer. "Time out" usually describes the process of having a child sit or stand apart from the rest of the class as punishment for a specific behavior or as a "cooling off" time.

Beyond the Question

Motivating students is always a challenge for teachers. Although effective teachers know that student motivation is essential to learning, they must also clearly understand their instructional goals. Can you articulate your overall goals for students before they graduate from elementary school?

In music: _____

In art: _____

In physical education: _____

Specification	Demonstrates knowledge of a variety of approaches to instruction and the theoretical and empirical bases of these approaches. (For example: developmentally appropriate instruction and model-based classroom management.)
2F	

About the Specification

Music, art, and physical education involve both cognitive and physical skills and development. What theories do you know that are relevant to the design of instruction in these content areas?

In music: _____

In art: _____

In physical education: _____

sample question

According to Piaget, children who are not yet in the "concrete operations stage" might have trouble in an art class that has group projects because these children have difficulty

(A) performing goal-directed actions

(B) manipulating materials to represent a vision

(C) engaging in a collective dialogue with their peers

(D) understanding that objects can exist whether one sees them or not

About the Question

How would you know that a student has not reached the "concrete operations stage"? _____

What is the answer? _____

Explanation of the Answer

As you have seen in earlier sample items, this test assumes that you are familiar with the theories of the Swiss psychologist Jean Piaget. If you are not conversant with Piaget's work, and with how it can be applied in classroom teaching, you should study his theories before you take this test. A brief summary is provided below.

(C) is the correct answer. Children who are not yet in the "concrete operations stage" are not likely to be able to engage in a collective dialogue with their peers.

Piaget studied the cognitive development of children and, based on his observations, he theorized that humans develop cognitive skills in stages and that all people progress through four stages, always in the same order. These stages are described very briefly here.

Sensorimotor: from birth to age 2.

A child's cognitive system is limited to motor reflexes at birth, but children build from these reflexes and begin to generalize their cognitive skills to a range of situations.

Preoperational Thought: from 2 to 6+ years.

Children acquire representational skills in the areas of language and mental imagery. However, they remain focussed on themselves and can only use their representational skills to see the world from their own point of view.

Concrete Operations: from 6+ to 11+ years.

Children in this stage are able to take another's point of view and see more than one perspective simultaneously. They can understand concrete problems but not abstract ones, and they are not able to consider a range of logically possible outcomes for situations.

Formal Operations: from 11+ to adult.

Children who reach this stage can reason theoretically and can think logically and abstractly. They use these skills, with increasing fluency, throughout adulthood.

 Beyond the Question

Piaget's research relates to the <u>cognitive</u> development of children. When planning instruction, teachers also have to be aware of the <u>physical</u> development of their students, especially in the areas of music, art, and physical education.

What theories of physical development do you know?

_____

_____

_____

How do these relate to planning instruction in these three content areas?

_____

_____

_____

Specification

3A

Demonstrate knowledge of when and how to use traditional and standardized testing methodologies. (For example: standardized tests, publisher-produced tests, screening tests.)

About the Specification

Will your students be required to take any standardized tests in music, art, or physical education in the state where you hope to teach? If so, what are the tests and at what grade level are they administered? _____

_____

_____

sample question

At the end of a unit, a music teacher wishes to determine whether students can explain three major influences on composers of the Romantic period. Which of the following tests would be the most appropriate to use?

(A) multiple choice

(B) essay

(C) portfolio

(D) performance

About the Question

What is the Romantic period in music? _____

_____

What are three major influences on composers of the Romantic period?

1. _____

2. _____

3. _____

What is the Answer?_____

Explanation of the Answer

Teachers should have a firm understanding of the various types of tests and their uses. This question asks you to identify which type of test is the most appropriate for determining whether students can <u>explain</u> three major influences on composers of the Romantic period. The key word here is "explain."

(B) is the correct answer. An essay gives students an opportunity to explain what they know, to demonstrate a deeper understanding of the material, to show relationships between concepts, and to analyze the information through clear thinking and writing. This would be the best way to determine whether students understood the influences that were discussed in this unit on Romantic composers. The other choices are all appropriate methods of evaluation, but not for this particular material.

Beyond the Question

What could the teacher evaluate about student understanding of the Romantic period in music using a multiple-choice test? _____

_____

What could the teacher evaluate about student understanding of the Romantic period using a portfolio? _____

_____

What could the teacher evaluate about student understanding of the Romantic period using a performance test? _____

_____

Specification 3B	*Demonstrate knowledge of various classroom-based, informal, or nontraditional assessment strategies. (For example: observation; oral reports; running records; informal reading inventories; portfolios; and performance samples.)*

About the Specification

What kinds of assessments listed in the specification are appropriate for assessing students in music? _____

_____

What kinds of assessments listed in the specification are appropriate for assessing students in art? _____

_____

_____

What kinds of assessments listed in the specification are appropriate for assessing students in physical education? _____

_____

sample question

A music teacher has taught several thematic units throughout the marking period. Which of the following is LEAST appropriately assessed by portfolios?

(A) students' responses to musical selections

(B) influences on composers studied by students

(C) comparisons of major musical trends

(D) musical notes on the bass clef

About the Question

Three of the four possible answers show appropriate ways of using portfolios in assessing students' understanding of what they have learned in music. Can you think of other topics in music that might be assessed by portfolio?_____

_____

_____

What is the Answer? _____

Explanation of the Answer

The portfolio is a useful type of non-traditional assessment, but it is not appropriate in certain situations. Here you are to identify a music unit that is LEAST likely to lend itself to portfolio assessment.

(D) is the correct answer. In order to assess students' understanding of musical notes on the bass clef, a teacher might use a performance sample or a similar method that allows students to demonstrate their knowledge. Portfolios generally contain students' work over a period of time. They allow the teacher and student either to see the progress made by the student or to see the best work by the student in a subject.

The other choices are all better suited to assessment by the portfolio method.

Beyond the Question

The kind of assessment you use is determined by what it is you want to assess. Pick either the upper-elementary or lower-elementary level and think about the skills and knowledge appropriate for those students in music, art, and physical education. How would you assess these?

<u>Level:</u>   <u>Lower Elementary</u>   <u>Upper Elementary</u>   (circle one)

<u>*Music Knowledge and Skills*</u>	<u>*Assessment Methods*</u>
_____	_____
_____	_____
_____	_____

<u>*Art Knowledge and Skills*</u>	<u>*Assessment Methods*</u>
_____	_____
_____	_____
_____	_____

<u>*Physical Education Knowledge and Skills*</u>	<u>*Assessment Methods*</u>
_____	_____
_____	_____
_____	_____

Specification

3C | *Interpret data obtained from various formal and informal assessments.*

About the Specification

Because art, music, and physical education often involve actual performance, the "data" you receive from assessments may be different from data in other subjects. For example: if students produce clay sculptures after discussing artistic approaches to sculpture, their sculptures become "data." What assessment techniques might you use to assess works of art produced by students?

_____

_____

_____

An elementary physical education teacher is interested in determining whether or not the students meet the criteria for an underhand volleyball serve. The criteria are:

● the server does not step over the line

● the server hits the ball with the correct motion

● the ball clears the net and goes into fair play

Which of the following is the best form of evaluation for this teacher to determine whether students meet the criteria?

(A) written test

(B) portfolio assessment

(C) teacher observation checklist

(D) student journal

About the Question

Students (and parents) might ask how the teacher ensured fair and consistent evaluation of this physical education activity. If you were the teacher, how would you respond to your students (and their parents)? _____

What is the Answer? _____

Explanation of the Answer

Assessment of student mastery takes many forms. Effective teachers are able to select the most appropriate form of assessment for the activity they want to evaluate. Here a physical education teacher has a list of three criteria that indicate mastery of the underhand volleyball serve. You are asked to identify the form of evaluation that is most appropriate for the task. Although teachers should be familiar with all four forms of assessment, they should also know when each is most likely to be useful.

(C) is the correct answer. With clear performance criteria in place for this physical activity, the teacher observation checklist is the most appropriate evaluative activity. None of the other options is likely to yield useful results.

Beyond the Question

You can see that making the evaluative criteria clear to all students, in advance of the assessment, is essential. The teacher in this example was very specific about what constituted "success."

What evaluative criteria might you use to assess students' performance in singing?

_____

_____

Specification **3D**	Identify common points of confusion or misconceptions among elementary school learners in the various content areas. (For example, errors and patterns of error; inaccurate factual knowledge or vocabulary; misconceptions about processes or relationships; "buggy" algorithms.)

About the Specification

Students frequently have misconceptions about subjects they are studying in school. It is reasonable to assume that they are confused about concepts in music, art, and physical education, just as they are confused about concepts in other content areas. Choose a grade level that you would like to teach and see if you can identify ways in which students at that level might be confused.

Grade Level: _____

What misconceptions might students have about music? _____

_____

What misconceptions might students have about art? _____

_____

What misconceptions might students have about physical education? _____

_____

sample question

After teaching a unit on symmetry, an elementary art teacher informally assessed the class and found that a significant number of students had difficulty understanding the concept. The teacher then discussed symmetry in new ways, answered students' questions, and asked the students to write a short description of symmetry. The art teacher was doing all of the following EXCEPT:

(A) promoting student comprehension

(B) evaluating and refining instruction

(C) teaching for understanding

(D) using standardized tests

About the Question

What are some techniques that the teacher might have used to clarify common points of confusion? _____

_____

What is the Answer? _____

Explanation of the Answer

Effective teachers recognize that simply teaching a new concept is not enough. They know that they must find ways to assess students' understanding of the concepts that they believe they have taught. "Teaching for understanding" is a critical component of teaching. If students do not fully understand a new concept, a teacher must "re-teach" the concept in new ways and then re-assess student understanding. The teacher in this example is doing exactly that.

(D) is the correct answer. The teacher is not using standardized tests to assess student understanding. Standardized tests are not always the best way to evaluate what students know, and effective teachers utilize a number of techniques to discover what their students understand and what they still need to learn.

Beyond the Question

The teacher in the question above uses the original "informal" assessment for information about her students' understanding, and for informing further teaching. What informal assessment techniques might the teacher have used to determine what students knew (and didn't know) about symmetry?

_____

_____

_____

_____

PUTTING IT ALL TOGETHER

ARTS AND PHYSICAL EDUCATION

Now that you have worked through this section of the workbook, you should have a general idea of what curriculum, instruction, and assessment issues are likely to appear on the test. The following chart is intended to help you think about the areas in which you might need further review before you take the test.

In addition, here is a list of topics that might appear on the test in the context of curriculum, instruction, and assessment in this subject area. Can you answer questions on these topics?

Sample Topics

- Knowledge about and appropriate activities for music and art education

- Basic concepts in music and art: rhythm, melody, harmony, and timbre in music; design in art

- Teaching strategies to encourage creativity and appreciation in music and art

- Music and art in other cultures

- Design of appropriate art and music activities for various developmental levels

- Classroom and playground safety

- Value of games and sports

- Design of appropriate physical education activities for various developmental levels

- Body coordination, movement, and movement exploration

If you are working in a study group, you might try asking each other questions on these topics. You might also challenge each other to come up with questions based on the topics and on the specifications that appear throughout this section.

STUDY PLAN: ARTS AND PHYSICAL EDUCATION

Content areas I need to study	Materials I have	Materials I need	Where can I find material I need?

GENERAL KNOWLEDGE | *Curriculum, Instruction, Assessment*

6

Specification **1A**	*Identify broad purposes for teaching all content areas and identify purposes for teaching particular topics within each content area.*

About the Specification

Why do we, as citizens, send our children to elementary school? What skills and knowledge do we, as a society, believe that children should develop in the elementary school years?

_____

_____

_____

sample question

An elementary school teacher wants students to become life-long readers. Which of the following is LEAST likely to help achieve that goal?

(A) giving students a choice of books to read for a book report

(B) providing students with time each day to read a book of their own choosing

(C) assigning each student an author about whom they are to read a biography

(D) reading aloud books that are interesting and exciting, even if some are above grade level

About the Question

What do you believe motivates students to want to read? _____

_____

_____

What is the assumption in this question, and the possible answers, about what motivates students to want to read?_____

_____

_____

What is the Answer? _____

Explanation of the Answer

Both short and long-term purposes of instruction are readily understood by successful teachers. They have a strong sense of how the curriculum fits together across content areas as well as within them. Here you must determine which strategy is LEAST likely to help students "become life-long readers."

(C) is the correct answer. By assigning an author, the teacher has taken away "choice," and this often leads to students being less enthusiastic about their reading. The other options include student choice and books that are "interesting and exciting." As you can see, the question and possible answers assume that students are less motivated to read if they are simply assigned books to read.

Beyond the Question

The question above asks about motivating children to continue to use their reading skills after their formal schooling has ended. What other skills do children develop in elementary school that teachers should promote as "skills for life"? (You might want to see how these relate to your answers to the first questions above, under the heading "About the Specification.")

_____

_____

_____

 Specification **1B** *Understand the relationship of subject area "parts" to subject area "wholes" for instructional planning and the instructional implications of these relationships.*

About the Specification

What would this specification mean for planning an integrated curriculum for the school year in a class you hope to teach?_____

_____

_____

What are some of the factors a teacher must consider when planning an integrated curriculum for the school year at any grade level?_____

_____

_____

---

sample question

The theories of the Swiss psychologist Jean Piaget have implications for planning curricula in all of the following areas EXCEPT

(A) understanding how children think

(B) using concrete materials in teaching

(C) constructing a rich social environment

(D) sequencing instruction appropriately

About the Question

What aspect of child development most interested Piaget? _____

What is the Answer? _____

Explanation of the Answer

In every subject area, teachers must understand how to plan curricula so that students are most likely to learn. To do this, they must understand how children comprehend and how they develop intellectually. Here you are asked about the applications of the theories of Jean Piaget, whose work you are expected to know.

(C) is the correct answer. Piaget's theories, based on observations of children, have implications for understanding how children think, how to use concrete materials in teaching, and how to sequence instruction. They do not have bearing on how to construct a rich social environment.

Piaget studied the cognitive development of children and, based on his observations, he theorized that humans develop cognitive skills in stages and that all people progress through four stages, always in the same order. These stages are described very briefly here.

Sensorimotor: from birth to age 2.

A child's cognitive system is limited to motor reflexes at birth but children build from these reflexes and begin to generalize their cognitive skills to a range of situations.

Preoperational Thought: from 2 to 6+ years.

Children acquire representational skills in the areas of language and mental imagery. However, they remain focussed on themselves and can only use their representational skills to see the world from their own point of view.

Concrete Operations: from 6+ to 11+ years.

Children in this stage are able to take another's point of view and see more than one perspective simultaneously. They can understand concrete problems but not abstract ones, and they are not able to consider a range of logically possible outcomes for situations.

Formal Operations: from 11+ to adult.

Children who reach this stage can reason theoretically and can think logically and abstractly. They use these skills, with increasing fluency, throughout adulthood.

Beyond the Question

In considering the grade level you would like to teach, what are the implications of Piaget's findings for your curriculum planning?_____

_____

_____

Specification 1C	_Understand relationships among concepts both within and across content areas and the instructional implications of these interrelationships._

About the Specification

Name some concepts that carry across content areas at a grade level that interests you (for example, for upper elementary school the concept of "proportion" emerges in mathematics, science, and art).

Grade level: _____

_____

_____

Of the following, the best way to present the contributions of women of both the past and the present would be to

(A) invite important community resource people to speak on the roles of women in the workplace

(B) solicit classroom involvement by students' parents

(C) incorporate into as many subject areas as possible information about the accomplishments of women

(D) include at each grade level a social studies unit on famous women

About the Question

How does this question relate to the specification? _____

What is the Answer? _____

Explanation of the Answer

Both (A) and (D) treat the contributions of women as something out of the ordinary. (B) doesn't really provide an answer to the question but, nonetheless, often functions in the classroom as if it were an actual answer.

The correct answer is (C). One way to restate this answer would be: "Make the contributions of women a part of every curriculum." This is an issue that all teachers should take into account when planning a curriculum in any subject area.

Beyond the Question

Traditionally, the contributions of women and many other groups have been neglected or under-emphasized in elementary school curricula. Besides women, what other groups' accomplishments should be included in curricula?

_____

_____

_____

If you don't know how to incorporate the contributions of these groups, how might you find the information you need? _____

_____

_____

Specification

1D   *Identify types and uses of curricular materials, media and technologies, and other resources.*

About the Specification

What are "curricular materials"? _____

_____

In general, what materials are available in multimedia and electronic forms? _____

_____

---

sample question

All of the following are instructionally sound reasons for using a concept map EXCEPT

(A) to assess students' progress on writing a report

(B) to gauge prior knowledge of a topic

(C) to serve as a review before a test

(D) to function as an end-of-lesson, chapter, or unit evaluation

TIP: This question states that "All of the following are instructionally sound reasons . . . EXCEPT." That wording tells you that one of the options presented is NOT instructionally sound. This is the one that you are looking for; this is the answer. If more than one option seems to you not to be valid, choose the one that seems least valid. Remember that there are no "trick" questions on this test. In this type of question, there will be one answer that is not as valid as the others.

About the Question

What is a "concept map"? _____

_____

How is a concept map "curricular material"? _____

_____

_____

What is the Answer? _____

Explanation of the Answer

A "concept map" is a visual web or diagram of how concepts are related to each other. It is most useful as an instrument to assess students' understanding of major concepts or themes and can be used appropriately by teachers before teaching a new unit (to see what students already know) or at the end of a unit (to see what students have learned and what they have not yet mastered).

(A) is the correct answer. Concept maps can help teachers gauge prior knowledge; they can serve as a review before a test; and they can function as an evaluation at the end of a lesson, chapter, or unit. However, they are not useful for assessing students' progress when they are writing reports.

Beyond the Question

In addition to concept maps, what other innovative resources might teachers use in implementing a curriculum? _____

_____

_____

_____

INSTRUCTION

Specification 2A	Demonstrate knowledge of methods of identifying, assessing, activating, and building on the students' prior knowledge, experiences, cultural backgrounds, and skills in each content area.

About the Specification

As a teacher, how might you get to know your students?_____

_____

_____

As a teacher, what would you like to know about your students? _____

_____

What documents might be available to use for this purpose (including school documents, like student records; documents produced by students, like reports on their families; and any other kinds of documents)? _____

_____

_____

How could you use such information to help you plan instruction? _____

_____

How might teachers serve as resources for each other in getting to know students?

_____

In what ways might teachers learn from students themselves? _____

_____

sample question

All of the following are ways an elementary school teacher can accommodate differences in students' backgrounds and help students become successful EXCEPT

(A) assessing students' prior knowledge of topics to be taught

(B) leading discussions that build on common experiences of the students

(C) offering students opportunities to write about their family backgrounds

(D) focusing classroom discussions on a particular group of minority students

About the Question

What are some other ways to help students accept diversity among their classmates? _____

_____

What is the Answer? _____

Explanation of the Answer

American classrooms are becoming increasingly diverse. Students come from a wide range of backgrounds and bring with them a diversity of experiences, attitudes, and living situations. This provides a tremendous resource for elementary school teachers. Teachers have a vital role to play in helping their students tolerate and appreciate diversity. Classrooms should be "inclusive" environments, and teachers should work actively to promote acceptance. This question asks about appropriate ways for a teacher to accommodate difference.

(D) is the correct answer. All of the proposed activities are appropriate ways to accommodate difference, except focusing classroom discussions on a particular group of minority students.

Beyond the Question

Choices (A), (B), and (C) above are all considered ways of accommodating differences in students' backgrounds. However, a teacher might have a different purpose for employing each of these strategies.

What is an instructional purpose of choice (A), "assessing students' prior knowledge of topics to be taught"? _____

_____

What is an instructional purpose of choice (B), "leading discussions that build on common experiences of the students"? _____

_____

What is an instructional purpose of (C), "offering students opportunities to write about their family backgrounds"? _____

_____

Specification 2B	Demonstrate knowledge of methods of preparing, evaluating, and justifying instructional activities within and across content areas.

About the Specification

What constitutes a valid justification for an instructional activity?

_____

_____

_____

_____

A third-grade teacher is planning a social studies unit. The teacher will focus student work around a novel that includes descriptions of nature, American Indian culture, and wilderness survival techniques. This type of instruction is an example of which of the following?

(A) Diagnostic-prescriptive method

(B) Integration through thematic units

(C) Team teaching

(D) Empirical approach

About the Question

How might this teacher sequence instruction, as a means to guide students through the topics of nature, American Indian culture, and wilderness survival techniques?

1._____

2._____

3._____

What is the Answer? _____

Explanation of the Answer

Integrating the teaching of the curriculum is a goal for all elementary school teachers. Here a teacher is using a novel to discuss topics in social studies. You are asked to identify the type of instruction the teacher is demonstrating.

(A) is not the correct answer. "Diagnostic-prescriptive method" incorporates an assessment (a "diagnosis") and specific assignments ("prescriptions") based on the results of the assessment.

(B) is the correct answer. This is an example of "integration through thematic units." Integrating curricula should be a goal for teachers in elementary school.

(C) is not the correct answer. "Team teaching" refers to teachers working together with other teachers as part of a teaching "team."

(D) is not the correct answer. An "empirical approach" is one in which students work in a "hands on" fashion. A good example would be a science experiment, in which students draw conclusions from their participation.

Beyond the Question

What kinds of interdisciplinary activities might this teacher plan for students to make the unit meaningful? _____

_____

What are some assignments or activities that this teacher could design to link the themes of the book? _____

Specification 2C | *Select teaching and learning strategies to help individual students or groups of students understand topics and concepts within content areas.*

About the Specification

What factors determine the strategies that a teacher chooses for teaching a particular topic? _____

_____

Which of these are "student based"? _____

Which of these are "teacher based"? _____

sample question

Which of the following is NOT a primary goal of a cooperative-learning approach?

(A) Students will be motivated to help one another.

(B) Students will develop time management skills.

(C) Students will have a stake in one another's successful learning.

(D) Students will be able to explain what they are learning to other students.

About the Question

The possible answers describe some of the advantages of cooperative learning. What are some of the potential disadvantages? _____

_____

What is the Answer? _____

Explanation of the Answer

"Cooperative learning" describes a model for students effectively working together. Since it is usually the group's work as a whole that is graded or evaluated, students generally work together as a team. This approach generates many positive outcomes, several of which are addressed in this question. Three of the four possible answers describe goals of the cooperative learning approach. You are asked to identify the one that is NOT a primary goal.

(B) is the correct answer. Although the cooperative project may contribute to some students' development of time management skills, this is not a primary goal of this kind of instruction. All of the other options are goals of a cooperative learning approach.

Beyond the Question

Many parents (and some educators) are critical of cooperative learning because there are so many ways for it to be done badly, which often negates its possible positive outcomes. What are the responsibilities of the teacher in creating positive learning outcomes from a cooperative learning task?

_____

_____

Specification	Demonstrate knowledge of methods of adjusting instruction to meet students' needs.
2D	

About the Specification

How would you adjust your own instruction to meet the following student needs?

Low motivation_____

_____

Attention deficit disorder _____

_____

Limited English proficiency _____

_____

Gifted (skills above grade level) _____

_____

Early in the school year, a teacher who uses cooperative groups finds that one student in a particular group is too immature to work productively. The teacher could address this problem in the short term by doing which of the following?

(A) Limiting the amount of time the class spends in cooperative groups

(B) Increasing the number of children in this child's group to offset the lack of contribution from this child

(C) Working with this child individually as well as allowing the child to participate in the group

(D) Encouraging other children in the group to do this child's share of the work

About the Question

What actions by the student might cause the teacher to conclude that he or she is too immature to work productively in a cooperative group?

_____

_____

_____

What is the Answer? _____

Explanation of the Answer

Some children are not able to work well in cooperative groups and their behavior may affect the overall productivity of the group. This question asks how a teacher might best address such a problem in the short term.

(A) Limiting the amount of time the class spends in cooperative groups based on the behavior of one student is not the best solution.

(B) Increasing the number of children in the group is not likely to change the behavior of the student in question and is not the best solution.

(C) is the correct answer. Allowing the child to participate in the group is essential for the growth and development of the child, but this child will also benefit from individual work with the teacher—and so will the group.

(D) Encouraging other children in the group to do the work of the child in question is entirely inappropriate. It both stigmatizes the immature child and punishes the group for the child's actions.

Beyond the Question

How can the teacher structure the short-term solution (working with the student individually) so that he or she might achieve the longer-term goal of working cooperatively within the group? _____

_____

_____

What are some of the most important features of cooperative groups, as described by David and Roger Johnson? _____

_____

Specification	Demonstrate knowledge of various strategies for motivating
2E	students and encouraging their success. (For example: praise, wait time, token economies, and student choice.)

About the Specification

Teachers can't make students learn. Students must be motivated in order to learn. It follows, therefore, that teachers must know how to motivate students or they won't be successful in achieving their teaching goals (and students won't be successful in achieving the learning goals that teachers have for them). However, what motivates one student to learn may not motivate all students to learn; what motivates a particular student in one subject may not motivate that same student in a different subject. The challenge for the teacher is to know and to be able to apply motivational strategies that encourage students to choose to learn.

In what situations do you think that "token economies" might be effective motivators?

_____

How does the use of "praise" change depending on the grade level and age of students?

_____

---

sample question

 "Wait time" is most useful as a strategy when a student is

(A) not focussed

(B) thinking

(C) embarrassed

(D) speaking

About the Question

What is "wait time" and when is it most useful as a strategy?

_____

_____

What is the Answer? _____

Explanation of the Answer

"Wait time" can be an effective strategy for motivating students and encouraging their success. It is simple to implement. For example: a teacher can provide a little extra time for a child to answer a question aloud before explaining the answer or moving on to another student. This extra time can be just the time the student needs to formulate an answer to the question.

(B) is the correct answer. "Wait time" is often "thinking time." It allows students to comprehend a teacher's question and come up with an answer. Other strategies are more effective when students are not focussed, are embarrassed, or are already speaking.

Beyond the Question

What might be a useful strategy for a teacher to use when a student is not focussed? _____

_____

Specification	Demonstrates knowledge of a variety of approaches to instruction and the theoretical and empirical bases of these approaches. (For example: developmentally appropriate instruction and model-based classroom management.)
2F	

About the Specification

Imagine that you get a job as a first-grade teacher. What are some of the key concepts that first graders should be taught? Name at least one activity you would do with students to teach each concept.

Key Concept   _Instructional Activity_

_____

_____

_____

According to Howard Gardner's Theory of Multiple Intelligences, a student with high kinesthetic intelligence and low interpersonal and linguistic intelligences would be most likely to learn science concepts in which of the following ways?

(A) Discussing them with other students

(B) Finding ways to act them out

(C) Writing about them

(D) Reading about them

About the Question

What would a student with "high kinesthetic intelligence" and "low interpersonal and linguistic intelligences" be like?

_____

_____

What is the Answer? _____

Explanation of the Answer

Candidates for teacher licensing are expected to know Howard Gardner's Theory of Multiple Intelligences and to be able to apply the theory in the classroom. Here you are asked about effective instructional approaches to teaching science concepts to a learner with high kinesthetic intelligence and low interpersonal and linguistic intelligences.

(B) is the correct answer. Kinesthetic learners are most likely to learn from acting out the concepts being taught. Discussing, writing, and reading are approaches that are not likely to be as successful with kinesthetic learners.

Beyond the Question

What would the strengths and weaknesses of the student described in the question above be in learning new material?

Learning Strengths   *Learning Weaknesses*

_____   _____

_____   _____

_____   _____

Specification	Demonstrate knowledge of when and how to use traditional
3A	and standardized testing methodologies. (For example: standardized tests, publisher-produced tests, screening tests.)

About the Specification

What kinds of general standardized tests do students in your state have to take during elementary school? _____

_____

_____

To whom are results of these tests reported? _____

If you have not already seen these tests, how might you be able to see them or to learn their structure and content? _____

_____

sample question

Criterion-referenced methods of reporting student achievement are based on

(A) a score that compares each student's score with the scores of other students in the same class

(B) a score that compares each student's score to that of a national group that has taken the same test

(C) the number of questions each student answered correctly for given objectives

(D) each student's standing in relation to others who took the test in terms of grade and month in the school year

About the Question

Define in your own words what "criterion-referenced" means. _____

What is the Answer? _____

Explanation of the Answer

Prospective teachers are expected to understand testing methodologies. This question asks about the meaning of "criterion-referenced" methods of reporting student scores.

(A) A score that compares a student's score with the scores of other students in the same class is said to be "norm-referenced."

(B) A score that compares a student's performance to a national group that has taken the same test is said to be "nationally norm referenced."

(C) is the correct answer. "Criterion referenced" refers to a test in which the correct answers by category are calculated against objectives.

(D) Comparing a student's standing in relation to others in the same grade and same month in school is referred to as "developmentally referenced."

Beyond the Question

Many states now test elementary-school students to see if they meet state standards in various subjects. The tests they use are criterion referenced, with the standards serving as the criteria. This is why it is important for you to know the standards for student learning in your state and to know as much as possible about the tests used to assess student learning. In addition to knowing the criteria the tests are designed to measure, you should know their formats (multiple-choice, short answer, essay, etc.) and how long students are given to complete each section of the tests.

If you don't know about which tests are required in the state(s) where you want to teach, how might you find out? _____

_____

Specification 3B	Demonstrate knowledge of various classroom-based, informal, or nontraditional assessment strategies. (For example: observation; oral reports; running records; informal reading inventories; portfolios; and performance samples.)

About the Specification

Of the examples listed in the specification, list below any you do not know, and then indicate where you might find more information about each.

Assessment Strategy   *Sources of Information*

_____   _____

_____   _____

_____   _____

Which one of the following types of portfolios is generally considered to present the most accurate picture of a student's progress and development over time?

(A) working portfolio

(B) showcase portfolio

(C) record-keeping portfolio

(D) teacher portfolio

About the Question

What are these types of portfolios? In your own words, give a brief description of each below.

Working portfolio _____

Showcase portfolio _____

Record-keeping portfolio _____

Teacher portfolio _____

What is the Answer? _____

Explanation of the Answer

Portfolios are useful tools for both students and teachers. Different types of portfolios serve different purposes, however, and teachers must understand the uses of each. Here you are asked which type of portfolio provides the most accurate picture of student progress and development.

(A) is the correct answer. A "working" portfolio is generally considered to be the most accurate because it contains all of a student's work to date in a specific subject. It allows both the teacher and the student to see the progress that has been made and to identify areas in which the student still needs to develop.

(B) A "showcase" portfolio usually contains a student's best work in a subject. Since less successful work is excluded, the showcase portfolio does not provide the most accurate picture of a student's progress over time.

(C) A "record-keeping" portfolio usually refers to a portfolio kept by the teacher for each student with contents such as notes from the student's parents and anecdotal records taken by the teacher based on observing the student.

(D) A "teacher" portfolio usually describes a portfolio kept by the teacher which includes assignments given to the class, along with data on student performance and notes about the success of each assignment.

Beyond the Question

If you collected your students' working portfolios at the end of the first semester, what process would you use for evaluating them? _____

_____

What feedback might you give to students in your evaluations?_____

_____

What would be some benefits of students doing self-assessment on their own portfolios?

_____

Specification | *Interpret data obtained from various formal and informal assessments.*

3C

About the Specification

Data interpretation can range from interpreting a standardized score report to evaluating student portfolios, as described in the question for Specification 3B.

What kinds of data interpretation do you think that you need to learn more about?

_____

Where can you find the information you need?

_____

sample question

A second-grade teacher determines that all of the students in the class received a score of 50% or below on a norm-referenced science test. Which of the following is the best description of the basis of these results?

(A) The students' scores are based on their own degree of success in completing certain prescribed tasks.

(B) The students' scores are based on comparison with standards determined by testing a selected pool of individuals.

(C) The students' scores are based on the performance of a task in real life.

(D) The students' scores are based on anecdotal records kept by the teacher.

About the Question

Describe in your own words what "norm-referenced" means.

What is the Answer? _____

Explanation of the Answer

In order to be better able to interpret data from all types of assessments, teachers should be familiar with basic assessment terminology. Here a teacher receives scores for students on a "norm-referenced" science test. You are to determine the basis of these results.

(A) Student scores based on success in completing certain prescribed tasks come from criterion-referenced assessments.

(B) is the correct answer. Norm-referenced tests are judged in comparison with standards determined by testing a selected group of people: the standardized sample.

(C) Student scores based on the performance of a real-life task, or a situation closely matching real-life, are from "authentic" assessments.

(D) Student scores based on anecdotal records kept by the teacher are often part of a portfolio or other alternative assessment.

Beyond the Question

Assessment is not an end in itself. Perhaps the most important thing about assessment is interpreting and using the data once it has been collected. In the question above, what conclusions might the teacher draw about the students' performance on the norm-referenced test? _____

_____

What would you advise the teacher to do after reviewing the results of the test?

_____

Why? _____

Specification | Identify common points of confusion or misconceptions among elementary school learners in the various content areas.
3D | (For example, errors and patterns of error; inaccurate factual knowledge or vocabulary; misconceptions about processes or relationships; "buggy" algorithms.)

About the Specification

What might a teacher learn from studying patterns of errors made by students?

---

sample question

A small group of second-grade students is reading a story together aloud. One of the children has difficulty reading the word "sparkled." To make sure that all of the students understand the word, the teacher asks that student to read the rest of the paragraph aloud. Then, when the student has finished reading, the teacher asks the group: "How did the character in the story feel as she spoke, and what did her eyes do to show her excitement?"

The teacher is helping students to use which of the following word-comprehension strategies?

(A) phonic clues

(B) context clues

(C) configuration clues

(D) morphemic clues

About the Question

How does the teacher handle the student's difficulty with the unfamiliar word?

Why does the teacher ask the student who has difficulty with the word to read the rest of the paragraph aloud?

What is the Answer? _____

Explanation of the Answer

(B) is the correct answer. By focusing on the meaning of an unfamiliar word as it relates to the rest of the paragraph, the teacher is highlighting the use of context clues.

Beyond the Question

The question above shows that good teachers not only identify common misconceptions and errors, but also know how to adjust their teaching to help students comprehend, learn, and develop skills and strategies.

Name two common misconceptions or misunderstandings you know that elementary students often have. What methods of adjusting teaching do you know that might help students overcome their misconceptions and comprehend more fully?

Common Misconception   _Teaching Strategy_

_____   _____

_____   _____

PUTTING IT ALL TOGETHER

GENERAL KNOWLEDGE

Now that you have worked through this section of the workbook, you should have a general idea of what curriculum, instruction, and assessment issues are likely to appear on the test. The following chart is intended to help you think about the areas in which you might need further review before you take the test.

In addition, here is a list of topics that might appear on the test in the context of curriculum, instruction, and assessment in this subject area. Can you answer questions on these topics?

Sample Topics

- Knowledge and understanding about child development, learning theory, and students' problem-solving abilities

- Higher-order thinking skills

- Students' emotional and social development

- Evaluation of instructional effectiveness and of student progress

- Basic concepts of measurement

- Classroom organization

- Language acquisition and nonstandard language use

- General principles of instructional planning, motivation, and student assessment

- Interactions with parents and colleagues

- General issues of professional growth

If you are working in a study group, you might try asking each other questions on these topics. You might also challenge each other to come up with questions based on the topics and on the specifications that appear throughout this section.

STUDY PLAN: GENERAL KNOWLEDGE

Content areas I need to study	Materials I have	Materials I need	Where can I find material I need?

NOTES

NOTES